Marriage In The **RED**

Marriage In The
RED

Transforming Your Marriage
One Color at a Time

Dr. Levi Skipper

WESTBOW
PRESS
A DIVISION OF THOMAS NELSON

WestBow Press books may be ordered through booksellers or by contacting:

WestBow Press
A Division of Thomas Nelson
1663 Liberty Drive
Bloomington, IN 47403
www.westbowpress.com
1-(866) 928-1240

ISBN: 978-1-4497-0372-1 (sc)
ISBN: 978-1-4497-0374-5 (dj)
ISBN: 978-1-4497-0373-8 (e)

Library of Congress Control Number: 2010932297

Printed in the United States of America

WestBow Press rev. date: 07/19/2010

Contents

Foreword:

Have you ever wished that navigating a marriage was as easy as driving a car? I have. Think about it. The most basic car has a dashboard filled with gauges that monitor the condition of your car: a heat indicator lets you know if you are about to 'boil over,' an RPM dial alerts you to an over-stressed engine, a dropping oil level lets you know about possible leaks, a battery charge indicator makes you cognizant of available energy, the speedometer indicates just how fast you are going, and lastly, the fuel gauge tells you how much further you can go. Really nice cars have a navigation system that gives you somebody to argue with! Watching these gauges carefully can lead to many years of carefree driving.

Dr. Levi Skipper gives us the closest thing to a *'marriage dashboard'* that I know of in his new book, *Marriage in the Red*. Dr. Skipper uses the power of an allegorical story to share the stages by color-coding them red, yellow, green and blue. Just like a dashboard that can help keep your car in good running condition, this dashboard will help keep your marriage on the road to fulfillment.

Each 'color code' gives practical advice on how to build a marriage that God can bless. The storyline will hold your interest and the principles you learn and employ will strengthen your bond with your spouse. I cannot think of a marriage that would not be enhanced by reading this book and applying its lessons.

My advice to you is to *Go Big Blue!*

Dr. Dwight "Ike" Reighard
Lead Pastor
Piedmont Church
Marietta, Georgia

PART ONE:

MARRIAGE IN THE RED

H e just sat there with a blank stare on his face melting into his chair. His demeanor could only be described as, well, desensitized. Although he had morphed into the chair beside his wife, clearly he was thousands of miles away. She was boiling! Her legs were crossed in lady-like fashion with her body turned just slightly showing her back to him. She was noticeably put out. Her left foot gave indication she had drunk too much coffee, or perhaps her patience was wearing vitally thin. Without a word, their body language told the story: this marriage was in the red.

Keenly aware this meeting would take up the better half of his afternoon, he settled in his chair with a cup of coffee. As he grabbed a pen and a yellow legal pad, he offered a silent prayer to the Lord, "Father, I think this marriage needs help. Give me wisdom and guidance to help them." He leaned back in his chair and asked them a leading question.

"Well, what's on your mind? What can I do for you?"

She rolled her eyes slowly toward the dead wood which sat on her left. Taking a deep, audible breath of disgust, she broke the thick silence. "Well, Pastor Schaeffer, I'll just be upfront with you.

Owen has no desire to be here. In fact, if it weren't for me this marriage would have ended four weeks ago. He should be glad we have children, or he would have been served divorce papers so fast his head would spin!"

Pastor Schaeffer repositioned himself in his seat after hearing the dreaded word "divorce". Just that morning he had read in his personal devotion Paul's letter to the church at Ephesus. Even as she spoke, the Scripture, like a marquis flashing in his mind, went whizzing by:

Husbands love your own wives, just as Christ also loved the church and gave himself up for her, so that He might sanctify her, having cleansed her by the washing of the water with the Word.--Ephesians 5:25-26

He refocused his attention back on Norah as she continued to vent.

Her voice seemed to grow louder with every syllable. She was firing words at her husband which seemed to bounce off the invisible wall which had been erected between them. Pastor Schaeffer held his hand up just a couple of inches above his desk so as to calm her down. His phone buzzed which gave temporary relief from what he knew was about to happen.

"Pastor, you have a call on line one."

"Marlene, I am going to have to ask you to hold all my calls this afternoon. If my wife calls, you can put her through, but other than her, take a message and I'll get back in touch with them."

Marlene turned a bit red from embarrassment. She knew Pastor Schaeffer had Owen and Norah in his office, but she had completely forgotten. The phones that day seemed to ring without end.

"I am so sorry Pastor; it totally slipped my mind they were in the office with you. I'll be sure to hold your calls."

"No problem, Marlene." With an apologetic look, he turned back toward the disgruntled couple. "Sorry about that. The office has been overwhelmingly hectic this entire week. So let's get back to our discussion. Owen, what's going on?"

"Norah is losing her mind." She furrowed her brow and starred a hole of hatred right through him. "She has it in her head that I am cheating on her."

"Are you?" Pastor Schaeffer questioned quite abruptly.

With a defensive voice he almost shouted, "No! I am not cheating on her! She is all fired up because she found a few e-mails which I have exchanged on my blackberry with a co-worker."

"We used to have lunch together every Thursday. Now he's too busy at work. Yet he seems to have plenty of time to e-mail back and forth to what's-her-name."

Turning his full attention to Norah, Owen said, "Well the last six times we went out to eat, all you did was nag me! Pastor, isn't there a verse in the Bible somewhere that talks about a nagging wife?" He reached over and patted the Bible on the desk. Norah's temperature went through the roof, and she turned to face Owen straight on.

"Okay, okay. Let's settle down here for just a minute," said Pastor Schaeffer decisively. "Let me tell you what I have picked up on so far. It really is plain to see: your marriage is *in the red.*" He leaned back in his chair fully confident he had issued the proper color for their marriage. Their two heads twisted toward the Pastor and simultaneously their jaws dropped.

"What are you talking about?" Owen questioned. They looked back at each other dazed, confused, and uncomfortable; agreement was a lost art in their relationship. They were both concerned about Pastor and his label of their marriage.

He chuckled a little bit and began to explain, "I see it all the time. The circumstances are slightly different, and the faces are always different, but the color is always the same: R-E-D." He had now actually spelled it out to them.

"You got my attention. Now tell me what you're talking about. What does it mean to be. . . *red*?" Norah asked.

He reached into his desk and pulled out a manila folder which had written across the top in all caps: MARRIAGE IN THE RED. After laying the folder down on his desk, he began to expound, "Your marriage can be red, yellow, green or blue. On one occasion I counseled a businessman about his marriage. He had made some colossal mistakes and was on the verge of giving up. We began our discussion one day over a cup of coffee, not about his marriage, but about his workplace. He explained to me how he was chosen to be on a team which would travel the country and do assessments of other businesses. They would rate each team they assessed using the four colors: red, yellow, green, or blue."

He took a sip of his coffee and continued, "If the team working was in the red, they were two months behind schedule. If they were in the yellow, they were one month behind. The green meant they were right on schedule. However, the coveted blue meant they were a month ahead and doing a superb job. " He continued with great confidence, "We have seen a massive increase in productivity as a result of this assessment tool."

Norah and Owen were paying attention, but still confused about what a color assessment chart for a business plan had to do with their marriage. But just before they would tune Pastor Schaeffer out he said, "I leaned over that day in the restaurant and with a unique God-given boldness, asked the highly intelligent and affluent business man, 'So what color is your marriage?' You could actually see the sting of God's conviction fall upon him at that moment. He quietly and truthfully said to me, 'It's in the red, Pastor; it's in the red.' "

Norah and Owen, practically on the edge of their seats, wanted to know what in the world being *in the red* meant. Owen finally just blurted out, "All right, Pastor. You have my attention. What does it mean to be *in the red?*"

"Unfortunately, I won't have time to share it all with you today." He reached in the manila folder and pulled out a single sheet of paper. He then tore a sheet of yellow legal paper off his notepad and began to draw as he spoke. "Couples in the red build invisible walls between themselves." He drew two stick figures on the paper. As he finished up the second stick figure, he began to draw long hair on it.

Owen smirked, "That isn't supposed to be Norah, is it? Way too skinny."

With a huge surge of righteous indignation coursing through his veins, Pastor Schaeffer quickly cut his eyes toward Owen. He clinched his jaws and said with a stern voice which neither of them had ever heard before, "Don't you ever talk ugly about your wife."

You would have to be from a different planet not to know Pastor Schaeffer meant business. In fact, the smirk on Owen's face disappeared. After what seemed like an awkwardly long stare, Pastor Schaeffer went back to drawing.

"Do you see the wall between you two here?" He pointed at the paper. Both Norah and Owen looked at the picture, but there wasn't a wall between the two at all. In fact, he hadn't even drawn a wall. "You can't see the wall, can you?"

They both responded, "No. Can you?"

"Well, if you could see the wall, then it wouldn't be invisible, would it?" That corny statement was perfect timing because it broke the tension which still filled the room after Pastor's rebuke of Owen's comment. "Now let me draw the outline of the wall."

Trying to save face after his former embarrassment, Owen spoke up, "I see it now, Pastor." Norah rolled her eyes; she knew what he was doing.

"Norah, what do you think needs to happen to help this marriage?" asked Pastor.

"I anticipated that question," she responded with a strong voice. "This is what I need if this marriage is going to work. Owen is going to have to stop flirting with girls in the office. He also needs to help do things at home. All he ever does is come in from work, sit down on his chair, and watch television. He doesn't play with the kids. I can't remember the last time he helped put up a dish or bathed one of the children. He just sits there. And he needs to talk to me, not his=pardon my French=Pastor, sluttish women down at the office. I'll tell you what else he needs to do. . ."

Owen sank into his chair and used his hand to jester a talking puppet which was directed at Norah's comments. Pastor Schaeffer interrupted, "Let's give Owen an opportunity to speak."

"Well, if Norah would hang out with me like she used to... We used to play tennis every weekend. We even played board games practically every other night. I mean, good grief, seems like she is ready to play a grungy game of tennis anyway: she always has her hair pulled back and her sweats on." He stopped, remembering the former rebuke of his Pastor. Giving just a slight pause for Pastor to speak up and noting that he didn't, he continued. . .

"All I ever get is a cold shoulder. She gives me the cold shoulder when I come in from work. She gives me the cold shoulder in the hallway. And not to mention, she gives me the very, very, very cold shoulder in the bedroom. If you know what I mean?" Then he thought to himself, "Does the Pastor know or even understand what I mean?"

"I know what you mean, Owen. I am a Pastor not an alien," Schaeffer replied sarcastically. He took his pen and pointed back at the outline of the invisible wall which he had drawn. "You would never have seen this wall had I not pointed it out for you on this paper."

"Invisible walls are built up in a marriage when both the husband and the wife believe every problem lies at the feet of the other. What happens then is simple. You slowly become bitter toward one another. Instead of dealing with your issues, you stuff them down in your heart and become bitter. The next step in bitterness is always hatred. Then anger, then outbursts of anger, resentment, and even malice in some cases." Within the parameters of the invisible wall he wrote each word as he spoke about it.

"When I asked you both to speak just a moment ago, did you not notice all you did was point a finger at each another? That is the tell-tale sign of a marriage which has constructed invisible walls. When your marriage is in the red, you never take time to look in the mirror. You are always looking out the window. In other words, you look out the window and become hyper-sensitive to the faults in your spouse. Yet you never look in the mirror and see the huge plank in your own eye."

"Marriage in the red," explained Pastor, "is a marriage built of invisible walls. Your greatest problem," as he looked at them both knowingly, "is that you are so busy trying to change one another that you haven't even considered the fact that *you* need to change."

Pastor Schaeffer reached over for his Bible which was tattered and torn. It was apparent he spent a great deal of time studying the Scriptures. He opened, not to the nagging wife passage, but rather to Paul's letter to the church at Colossae. "Paul is encouraging those within the church to get dressed." He began to read:

But now you also, put them all aside: anger, wrath, malice, slander and abusive speech from your mouth. Do not lie to one another, since you laid aside the old self with its evil practices, and have put on the new self who is being renewed to a true knowledge according to the image of the one who created him.--Colossians 3:8-9

"Norah and Owen, you both have received Christ as Lord; however, this does not mean everything is going to be perfect in this life nor in this relationship. You both will continue to battle your old nature, the flesh. The consequence of your sin nature was death. Jesus paid for that on your behalf through His death and resurrection."

Pastor Schaeffer continued, "A discipline of the Christian life is to learn how to dress properly for life. Paul borrowed a term from Greek culture which means to *take off your old clothes*. He says in essence, 'Before you met Christ, you used to wear anger, wrath, slander, and abusive speech. You used to wear lies and other evil practices. But now you have met Christ! You now dress completely differently. Get rid of those old clothes.' "

After a couple seconds of silence, Pastor Schaefer made a comment which neither of them would soon forget, "You can't expect your marriage to be godly if you are dressing up like the devil every day."

Both Norah's and Owen's eyes hit the floor. Pastor Schaeffer offered up another silent prayer. "Please, Father, protect them from the evil one. He would love to steal this word from their hearts before they leave this office. May Your word be implanted in them and bear a life of godliness." He caught their attention by saying, "Listen to what Paul tells us to put on:

> So, also those who have been chosen of God, holy and beloved, put on a heart of compassion, kindness, humility, gentleness, and patience, bearing with one another, and forgiving each other, whoever has a complaint against anyone; just as the Lord forgave you.--Colossians 3:12-13

"You see," Pastor explained, "as a follower of Christ you really have two closets where you can choose to get dressed. With every temptation, trial, and test in your marriage you will instinctively choose how you want to dress. You will put on your old clothes and be ungodly and sinful. Or you will put on your new clothes and be godly and holy. So Owen, let me ask you a key question."

Owen looked up with a mixture of fear and anticipation.

"As the spiritual leader of the home, would you say you have been dressing from the closet of your old life or the closet of your new life in Christ?"

"Well, I never really thought about it like that. I would have to say the old closet."

Pastor then asked, "So, how is that helping your marriage?" A long silence followed.

"Norah, it's your turn. Which closet is it for you: old closet or new?"

"I am definitely getting dressed in the old closet."

With a smile on his face Pastor Schaeffer said, "Great. Now we are getting somewhere. You have both been living in sin. As a result, you are reaping exactly what you have been sowing. You need to repent of your sin and trust God to help you get dressed from the right closet. You also need to work on asking for forgiveness from one another."

He grabbed the manila folder, put his sheet back in, opened the drawer, and put the manila folder back in its place.

"Wait a minute. Aren't you going to help us?" Norah asked. Pastor Schaeffer picked up his pen and began to write.

"I never let a patient leave without a prescription." He took the sheet of paper with the two skinny stick figures and the invisible wall and began to write under them.

Memorize Colossians 3:8-9, 12-13. Pray continuously for God to teach you how to get dressed. Come back and see me in a week.

"All right, before you leave, let me make sure I put you on my Google calendar. Let's pray and I'll see you guys soon."

CHAPTER TWO

They drove home in silence. Both of them felt the sting of conviction while listening to Pastor Schaeffer. However, neither of them would speak first. Like children after a squabble, they ignored one another for the entire fifteen minute ride home.

After he paid the babysitter, Owen retreated to his home office where he spent the majority of his evenings until late in the night. Norah was pleased to see both her children already bathed by the sitter. She was able to get them to bed a bit early and then unwind from the day in front of the television.

In the past year the scene in the house had not changed much. Owen would come in from work and heat up his supper. After eating by himself in front of the TV, he would withdraw into his fortress of solitude and surf the internet. Norah was always busy getting the kids ready for bed. Anyone with children knows how exhausting that task can be, especially when the kids are five and three. The only time they even saw one another was when Owen came out of his home office to get a snack in the kitchen. Or perhaps some nights when the kids knocked on his door to say good night, their paths would cross. If their eyes met, they would exchange a few cordials.

Norah was pretty confident that Owen was not surfing the web looking for better prices on groceries or playing fantasy football. He had forgotten one evening to delete his web history, and Norah was crushed by what she found. It seemed he had begun reading the local news online, but then he digressed to say the least. As she traced his internet steps, she was sickened and lessened by what she found. The web Owen allowed himself to be caught in caused great damage to his life of intimacy with Norah. She grew ill and empty.

Owen ceased to see his wife as his best friend and romantic lover. In fact, now all he saw in Norah was an irritating object. Not only this, the object he saw was unsatisfying to his own carnal eyes. His constant viewing of the internet caused him to begin comparing his wife to what he watched and desired online.

You can imagine how Norah felt, can't you? She felt worthless, ugly, unloved, and fat. She had never been overweight, but even her small glimpse of the internet filth had caused her to compare her body with those on the screen. As a result, she went on a strict diet and exercise regimen to try and catch Owen's eyes once again. However, she refused to be intimate with him. If he wanted to look at the web, then all he would be able to do is look at her too.

Norah joined a gym eight weeks prior to counseling with Pastor Schaeffer which gave her opportunity three nights a week to escape her house completely. After putting the children down around eight o' clock, she jumped in her car and headed out. Typically she would just speak through the door of her husband's office, "I'll be at the gym if you need me." Of course she knew he wouldn't be calling her. She felt he had lost all connection with her.

It was one Tuesday evening, five weeks prior to their session with Pastor Schaeffer, after she reached ten minutes on the treadmill that she spotted a guy across the gym. He looked overwhelmingly familiar to her. However, she had difficulty making him out due to the obstruction of the weight machine where he was sitting. He finally stood up and they made eye contact. After tilting his head a bit, kind of like a confused dog, he said, "Norah? Is that you?"

"Yeah," she said going through the rolodex in her mind trying to remember his name. Then it hit her, "Allen?"

"How have you been?"

"Just fine," she lied through her teeth. Of course it's not like she would open up and share that she and her husband had not been intimate in eight months.

"Last time I heard about you, someone told me you had another child."

"Yes, I have two children now," she pressed the stop button on the treadmill and picked up a towel to wipe the sweat from her face.

"Good for you," he said with a smile.

"What about you? Didn't you get married a few years ago?"

He looked at the floor and seemed a bit embarrassed. "I did. But it just didn't work out. We were divorced about six months ago."

"I am so sorry. I wouldn't have said a word if I had known." She felt terrible for Allen; he was always such a nice guy.

"No big deal. I have reached what my counselor calls the 'state of closure'. You know. . . where you basically get over it and move on with your life? It's great seeing you. Do you come in here and workout often?"

"Every Tuesday, Thursday, Saturday, and sometimes even on Sunday depending on how much ice-cream I had that weekend." They both laughed at her little joke. In fact, for Norah it felt both great and odd to laugh. She hadn't done that in a long time. She also mentally applauded herself; that was the first joke she had made in at least a year. When you are a house mom, your sense of humor is often unappreciated and unnoticed by children.

"Maybe I'll see you around then. I have to get back to the bench press machine. I have a weight lifting competition this weekend," he said sarcastically as he grabbed a roll of fat around his waste. They both laughed out loud and went back to their normal routine.

After seeing Allen that first night, she looked forward to his companionship each time she visited the gym. She even bought some new work-out clothes and would always make sure she had on lipstick, knowing she looked like death without it. Before long they began meeting each other at the treadmills around eight-thirty to just walk and talk. She found a unique satisfaction realizing he was looking for her and desired her attention. Norah found herself venting about her relationship with Owen most of the time. She wasn't looking for advice. She was just looking for someone to listen. Allen listened.

"Well, how was your day?" He asked at approximately 8:32 p.m.

"Yesterday we went to see our Pastor," Norah said.

"And. . . how did that go?"

"Well, Owen, sat there like a bump on a frog, or is it log, pretty much the entire time. Pastor Schaeffer basically told us we were both living in sin and getting dressed with our old life. Very encouraging, don't you think?"

"I never was a big fan of Pastors. Pretty much every one of them has problems, too, you know. I never could trust a Pastor. I always feel like they want me to give them some money. It's like they carry those offering plates in their back pockets or something. So how much is this Pastor Schaeffer charging you for the 'spiritual guidance'?" he asked with scorn in his voice.

"Pastor Schaeffer is a great man. I have been attending his church since I was in high school. I never once felt like he was trying to get any money out of me. Nor did he pass an offering plate to us after the session yesterday. He gave us a couple of verses we were supposed to memorize. She pulled a little note card out of her pocket and said the Bible verse address out loud, "Colossians 3:8-9, 12-13." Her eyes continued to scan the card as she silently read the verses.

"You mean he gave you a Bible verse? You went in there with a real problem, and he threw a Bible verse at you? Good grief! What kind of help is that?" Allen was clearly filled with animosity toward church and pastors.

"Yeah, just a few verses, but we have another meeting with him next week." Norah justified her Pastor's help.

"Promise me one thing. If you see an offering plate, run!" he said with a chuckle as he waved goodbye to Norah.

CHAPTER THREE

"You ready?" Owen's bellowing only caused Norah to roll her eyes. They were running a bit behind for their afternoon meeting with Pastor Schaeffer. They were both afraid he would ask them to quote the verses he gave the previous week. Neither of them had memorized the verses. However, the image of getting dressed with the old life or the new life, they couldn't erase.

Sitting in the car, he gave a quick blow of the horn to hurry her up. Norah came out frustrated and still putting on her left shoe. Again they rode in virtual silence to the church. As they pulled into the parking lot, Norah murmured under her breath, "Here we go again."

Pastor Schaeffer met them at the front door of the church. "How have you been doing this week? You have both been in my prayers. Owen, you look a little nervous. I'm not going to ask you to quote the memory verses, so just relax. Not this time anyway. Come on in and have a seat in my office. Would either of you like a cup of coffee?"

Owen responded, "I'll take a cup, please."

"I'm fine thanks," Norah said.

Looking at Owen, he asked "Cream or sugar?"

"No, thanks. Just black will be fine," Owen responded.

"All right. We have a real man with us now," Pastor Schaeffer said jokingly as he went back to the office break room to grab Owen a cup of coffee. As he poured the coffee, Schaeffer prayed, "Lord, give me wisdom with Owen and Norah and help me to lead them out of the red."

As he walked back into the office, he could still sense a bit of tension in the room. It was noticeable again by their body language, as it hadn't changed much over the past week. However, Pastor Schaeffer was still optimistic, relying upon God's power to intervene in due time.

As he handed the cup of fresh coffee to Owen, he began, "I want to start today by asking you both a question. How much time are you spending together? You know, one on one, just the two of you?"

Norah looked at Owen. Owen looked at Norah. And almost simultaneously they said, "None."

"Why aren't you spending any time with one another?" Pastor Schaeffer looked at Owen.

"Well, to be honest, when I get home from work I am dog-tired, and most of the time she is cleaning up and getting the kids to bed. Soon after that, she heads over to the gym to workout."

Not wanting to be viewed as an uncaring wife, Norah piped up, "Owen comes home, eats his dinner, and goes to his home office, and shuts the door. He is on the internet practically the entire night. He makes no effort to communicate with me or the children. He completely separates himself from any relationship with us whatsoever."

Pastor Schaeffer leaned back in his chair and asked, "So how long have you been looking at pornography, Owen?"

It was like the wind was sucked out of the room completely. Owen could feel his face turning blood red. Scrambling to find a response he said, "What kind of a question is that?"

"Look," Pastor Schaeffer said calmly, "this is not the first time I have counseled a couple who has had marriage problems. Usually when a wife makes a comment that her husband is *always on the internet* that is her way of letting me know--he's looking. Is that what you were trying to tell me, Norah?"

She feared her husband's reaction and was overwhelmingly embarrassed to be discussing pornography with a man of the cloth. She told herself she couldn't lie to a preacher in the church and thus justified her truthful response. "Let's just say I found plenty of evidence on the computer that he is venturing into territory he shouldn't be in."

Clinching his jaw out of anger and humiliation, Owen looked at the floor. This was much worse than getting your hand caught in any cookie jar.

Pastor Schaeffer then asked Owen a question off subject, "How does it make you feel when Norah leaves you at home to go work out?"

"Not good. I think what really gets on my nerves is how much money she is spending on new workout clothes. She used to just go in an old pair of sweat pants. Now half of our closet looks like a woman's sporting goods store. But, to answer your question, she is obviously avoiding me."

Pastor Schaeffer looked at Norah and asked, "Norah, do you work out by yourself, or are you meeting someone?"

She tilted her head back and furrowed her brow, and with frustration in her voice she said, "No, I'm not meeting anyone." Her voice grew louder. "All I am doing is working out, trying to get my husband to notice me again. Why are you asking me if I am meeting someone?" With smugness in her voice she repeated his question under her breath, "Am I meeting someone?"

Pastor Schaeffer sensed her defensive attitude. "Norah, I am not implying you are meeting someone. I was just curious."

He lifted up a silent prayer, "Lord, help me to not mess up here." He then began with a quiet but stern voice, "Norah, let me say upfront, I will not be able to help you at all unless there is total transparency in this office. So let me ask you that question again. Are you meeting someone where you are working out?"

"Well, I have not made any appointment to meet with anyone, no." Norah answered, carefully choosing her words. Owen slowly began to turn his head toward Norah. She could feel his eyes piercing him as she scratched her face.

"Okay?" Pastor said with a confused expression. "You aren't making an appointment . . . but there is someone at the gym that you speak with regularly, right?"

"I guess." Norah said embarrassed.

"You guess?" Pastor Schaeffer responded. "So what is her name?" He asked even though he was pretty sure her new friend wasn't a "she".

"His name is Allen. He is just an old friend from school. No big deal. It's not like I'm looking at porn!" she said looking squarely at Owen. "Besides, I can't very well ignore every person in the gym who isn't a lady. I mean, good grief, I'm married, not a recluse."

You could practically hear a gavel hit the judge's podium after Norah's statement of guilt. She wasn't having an affair with Allen, but she wasn't keeping her renewed friendship with him guarded either. Owen's anger was burning as he began to crack his knuckles. He turned his head to the right with his chin up and popped his neck. The only time Pastor Schaeffer ever saw a man look like that was right before he stepped into the UFC Octagon to fight.

"Owen, have you ever had a flat tire?" Pastor Schaeffer asked out of the blue. He wasn't A.D.H.D.; he just had a unique ability to turn everyone's attention to something else in order to make a valid point. This time was no different.

"Yeah, I came out to the parking lot once after picking up some groceries and my tire had gone flat."

"So it wasn't a blow out; it just slowly leaked out, right?" Schaeffer asked.

"Yeah, why? What does this have to do with anything?" Owen retorted impatiently.

"Over the course of many years, I have found marriages rarely are blow outs. Rather, they are small leaks which over time leave the marriage flat. You see," he drew their attention to him by leaning in and putting his hands on the desk, "your marriage has turned into a roommate situation more so than a romantic, godly relationship situation."

"When I was in college, I had a roommate who did his thing and I did mine. We shared expenses, the television, and air conditioning, but that was about all."

"So what does that have to do with Norah's boyfriend?" Owen asked with consternation in his voice, hoping his choice words cut Norah deeply.

Norah, not to be outdone or allow Owen to forget his sin, also asked, "Or his porn problem?"

Pastor Schaeffer pulled out a pen from his desk and began to write on a brand new sheet of yellow legal pad paper. Picking up from his drawing last week, he drew the two stick figures and the invisible wall between them. However, the stick figures were no longer facing one another but: rather, they were facing the opposite direction. Owen's stick man on the right continued to look toward the right. Norah's on the left was looking toward the left.

"You are in the red. You are living lives of complete independence. *You* are doing *your* own thing." He underlined Norah on the page with an arrow pointing to the left. "And *you* are doing *your* own thing." He underlined Owen with an arrow pointing to the right. "Where there are invisible walls, there will always be temptations to have outbursts of anger. When there is independence in the marriage, there is always a temptation to commit an affair."

Neither Norah nor Owen had ever believed they would commit affairs. In fact, as far as they knew, neither set of their parents had fallen morally either. An affair seemed so foreign to them they couldn't even imagine such a thing taking place.

"You guys remember the story of David and Bathsheba, right?" Pastor Schaeffer inquired as he opened his Bible. "In 2 Samuel 11 we read about David's moral failure:

> Now when evening came David arose from his bed and walked around on the roof of the king's house, and from the roof saw a woman bathing, and the woman was very beautiful in appearance.--2 Samuel 11:2

His spiritual gift of teaching began to kick in as he repositioned himself in the chair. Pointing at the Scripture he had just read, he remarked, "I am not completely sure what David's married life was like at this present moment. However, it is safe to say that David's activity at this moment was independent. When you begin to walk around looking for pictures or people to fill a void in your life, you are looking off the balcony like David."

"Owen, let's be honest; most men want sex." Both Norah and Owen's eyes looked surprised to hear the preacher say such a thing. "The truth is simple: sex is good between a married man and woman. However, your sexual desires will never be fulfilled if you are picturing internet women in your mind while you are intimate with your wife. Your sexual needs will never be fulfilled if you are comparing cyber-woman with your wife."

Turning his attention to Norah he called her out, "Norah, you want an emotional-relational connection with someone, but you can't find it walking out on the roof of life. Every time you leave home to work out, you are walking out on the roof looking for your Bath-*Allen*."

Pastor Schaeffer then looked at both of them and quite bluntly asked, "Have either of you committed adultery yet?"

Norah quickly said, "No," with Owen's response the same.

"I can assure you," Pastor Schaeffer looked back at his drawing, "if you continue in this direction, you will eventually fall."

A deacon from their church knocked on the door and poked his head in the office. "Pastor, I didn't think you were busy, so I figured I would pop in. But I see you have some folks with you." What makes some deacons always think the Pastor isn't busy?

Owen turned to see who had interrupted their session hoping they hadn't been listening through the door.

"Owen, what in the world are you up to?" The deacon enthusiastically asked. "Pastor, I have known Owen's father for almost thirty-five years. Owen, you will never meet a more godly man. In fact, at our Thursday morning prayer meeting he is always praying for you by name. Well, sorry to disturb. I'll talk to you later, Preacher. Have a good one."

After hearing how his father prayed for him every Thursday by name, Owen was hit by stinging conviction in his heart. Looking at Norah with Pastor's Schaeffer's profile in his peripheral vision, he felt sick thinking about his evenings in his office at home. "I can't believe I let my life come to this," he thought to himself.

"I'll talk to you later!" Pastor Schaeffer said to a closed door. The intruder had shut it as quickly as he had opened it. Schaeffer's words didn't escape the room. "Sorry about that." Pastor Schaeffer was slightly embarrassed for the lack of professionalism it displayed.

"All right, we have only about three minutes before my next appointment, so let me give you your assignment for this week."

"Did you say *assignment*?" Norah asked.

"We don't have to keep memorizing verses, do we?" Owen remarked.

"Owen, you need to stop looking at pornography. So I want you to bring me a receipt next week."

"A receipt?"

"I want you to go to Wal-Mart and purchase some software that will keep pornography from showing up on your computer. I want you to install it, but I want Norah to set the password." He began to jot on a post-it note the names of a few programs to choose from.

"How much will that program cost me?" Owen asked gruffly not desiring to spend any money.

Without even flinching Pastor Schaeffer handed him the post-it note and answered, "It won't cost you near as much as an affair."

"Norah, you need to cut off your relationship with Allen. I want you to join a different gym or start working out at the church gym. It's free and open to the public every weekday from 7:30 a.m. until 3:00 p.m. With the money you save, Owen can afford the program he needs to get for the computer."

He then asked Owen and Norah to join hands so they could pray. Owen reached over and Norah joined his hand reluctantly. They didn't interlock fingers. Owen held her hand as if Norah were his grandmother. Both of them thought about how weird it was to hold hands. In fact, Pastor Schaeffer had to say "Amen" twice to get them to let go. Not because they enjoyed it, but because they were both so mentally consumed with their hands touching they didn't even hear Pastor praying.

Pastor Schaeffer led them to the door. "See you next week at the same time. Memorize the Scripture I gave you and complete your assignments. We will get this marriage out of the red with God's help."

Pastor Schaeffer's next appointment was sitting in the waiting room just beyond his secretary. He asked him to head on back to his office and make himself comfortable. As the new appointment walked down the hall and Owen and Norah walked out the door,

Pastor leaned over to speak to his secretary. "Watch out for Deacon Ben. He practically burst the door down while I was counseling with Owen and Norah."

"Pastor, I am so sorry," she said. "I got up for like two minutes because Ms. Mary motioned for me down the hall, and he slipped right through. I think it's a conspiracy!" After sharing a laugh, Pastor Schaeffer went back to his office.

CHAPTER FOUR

The faint sound of Garth Brooks was coming from the radio as they drove home. Norah hated country music and usually demanded that the station be changed. This time she kept her mouth closed. Not because she chose to, but because she was thinking about Allen.

How was she to turn her back completely on Allen? How was she supposed to just quit going to the gym? Inwardly she began to justify reasons for why she could keep going to the gym. "I signed a contract that lasts a year," she thought. "I could go to the gym when I know he's not there."

Her mental gymnastics were interrupted by the blinker in the vehicle. Owen didn't have a silent blinker. His had an annoying ding, and even the side mirror would light up. His vehicle wasn't just letting people behind him know he was turning; it was designed to signal the world. It wasn't so much the sound that caught Norah's attention though; rather, it was the lighting up of the right side mirror. "Why is he turning into Wal-Mart?" she pondered.

"I am going to run into the store right quick. Do you need anything?"

"Why are we stopping at Wal-Mart? We need to hustle up, Owen. Lauri's mom will be there to pick her up in less than five minutes. You know she hates to wait." Norah exaggerated her baby-sitter's ride situation in order to get her point across. Her response to Owen was filled with frustration, not because of Wal-Mart, but because of Allen.

"I need to grab something. It won't take me but a few minutes. Do you need anything? Want to come in or sit here?" He asked.

"I'll just sit here and listen to Garth's greatest hits." she said rolling her eyes. "Surely he isn't going to get an internet filter." she thought.

He shut the door and disappeared behind the automatic doors of Wal-Mart. He asked the greeter at the door where the computer programs were located. The old man at the door put a yellow smiley face sticker on Owen's shirt and said with an overjoyed voice, "You look like you could use a smile! The computer programs-- I never could figure those things out. Whatever happened to a pencil and a sheet of paper?" he asked with a slight chuckle. He pointed to the right backside of the store and said, "I think I remember seeing them on aisle eight about the middle shelf. But, hey, don't put too much stock in what I say. I can't remember my birthday or where I live half the time." His smile was contagious and even spread to Owen.

"Thanks." Owen said while walking away with a Wal-Mart sticker on his shirt.

"Good luck with your computer programs. The pencils are on the aisle just in front of the computers."

Even though Owen had never put his eyes on the internet blocking software, it took him only a couple of seconds to find it. Picking the cheapest one he could find, he began walking toward the check-out lines. Holding the box of software while standing in line between two women, he became extremely embarrassed. Not to mention, he caught the lady behind him reading the label on the box. "Keep pornography away from your computer, for good, guaranteed."

"It's for our workplace." He said to the lady, lying through his teeth. "We have a few teenagers who love to surf the net." He added to his lie. He not only told her the story but embellished it while talking to the pregnant woman working the cash register. He even launched into how they had fired three teenagers before deciding to get the software. "We figured the software would be a good investment if it allowed us to keep our workers," he said with a grin on his face.

The automatic doors opened up, and Owen could see the back of Norah's head. He was tempted to toss the software into the nearest trash can in an effort to save face. Before he could spot a trash can, he saw Norah's eyes looking at him. He tried to act indifferent as he got back into the car.

He put the software just beneath his left leg while putting the car in gear. She knew that was a weird place for the bag, so she asked, "What you got?"

Without a word he reached under his leg with his left hand. Grabbing the bag, he handed it over to her without looking in her direction. She opened it and was stunned. Her thoughts of Allen escaped her mind temporarily. "You *actually* bought the software?" She said stressing the word "actually" and dragging it out for dramatic effect.

"You should know I am a type A personality. I am already behind on the memory verse. I can't let this assignment mess me up, too. Besides, isn't this what I was told to do?" He asked.

Silenced followed until they pulled into the driveway of their home. The kids were playing in the front yard, and Lauri was making sure they stayed back from the car until it stopped. Owen got out of the car and was met by Lauri's teenage voice, "Nice sticker, Mr. Owen!" He reached up and took the smiley face off his shirt and grinned a little thinking about the old man at Wal-Mart.

That evening Owen wasn't in his usual place. Sitting in the living room scanning the TV channels, he was looking for something to watch. He hadn't watched television at nine o' clock in the evening since. . . he couldn't remember when.

Norah had her workout clothes on and was tying up her new gel Asics. This time was different. She could feel the same weight of guilt on her shoulders as she did the first time she went to meet Allen. However, she had learned in the past how to ignore it. Pastor Schaeffer's discernment and direct speech caused her guilt to resurface.

Owen's head spun to the left as he heard the front door slam shut. Next he heard the sound of the car engine slowly disappearing into the night. "God, we really need some help here. If You are listening...forgive me. I really have royally messed up."

Owen ventured back into his home office, but not for his usual business. "There it is," he celebrated. It warmed his heart as he took the Bible his grandfather gave him five years ago for Christmas back into the living room. Turning off the television, he opened the Bible to the fly leaf where he re-read his grandfather's note. His grandfather dropped out of third grade and went right to work. His note was barely readable.

Owen,

I made hundreds of mistakes in this life. But God loves and Even longs to forgive. My favorite verse in the Bible is 1 John 1:9. Sure it will help you two.

Sadly, Owen remembered reading the note left by his grandpa but he had never read the verse. So he looked for 1 John, which took a while. After consulting the table of contents, he finally found page number 907. His eyes scanned down to the verse his grandpa loved.

After reading the verse he had to swallow a lump in his throat and actually fight back tears. Owen hadn't cried since middle school and had completely forgotten what it felt like. "Surely, I'm not going to cry over a verse in the Bible," he whispered to himself.

He had never felt such relief though. As he read the verse again, he just felt lighter. There is no other way to describe it. He felt as if he were losing weight:

If we confess our sins, He is faithful and just to forgive us our sins and cleanse us from all unrighteousness.—1 John 1:9

"God, I know you are there. Forgive me for ignoring You. I still remember the day you came into my life as a teenager. I used to be so on fire for You. I have gone off the deep end--like you don't already know. Now I just need You to cleanse me completely. Help me to be a better husband. Please help Norah." As he continued to pray he couldn't hold back the tears. In fact, the first tear which rolled off the end of his nose splashed right on the verse which had made such an impact on his grandfather and now on him.

Meanwhile Norah was on the treadmill filled with disappointment. "Where is he?" she thought to herself, a bit ill. Allen was usually on the treadmill next to her within ten minutes. Little did she know Allen's mother was rushed to the hospital after a terrible fall in her home a couple of days ago. As an only child to a widowed mother, he felt it necessary to spend twenty--four seven with her. Taking a couple vacation days, he ended up sleeping in a hospital recliner, which didn't recline. On top of that, the recliner was made of pleather, and every time he moved, it sounded like he passed gas. He had to apologize to two different nurses about the noise on more than one occasion. He also saw the two nurses whispering to one another in the hallway. He didn't think it had anything to do with him until he noticed that one dropped a bottle of air freshener into the pocket of her big white medical coat.

"There you are! Where have you been? I am almost through." she said desperately as she noticed Allen walking through the gym doors. He waved his hand but lacked his usual charming grin. The closer he got to Norah the worse he looked to her. "Are you okay?" She questioned.

"I have been in the hospital for forty-eight hours with my mom," he replied, rubbing his eyes, which were suffering from insomnia.

She felt terrible for her actions toward him and offered her apologies. "I am so sorry. What happened?"

"No, she'll be fine. She fell and broke her hip. She was trying to reach a towel in the cabinet above the toilet. She couldn't reach it, so she figured she would stand on the toilet seat to get a lift. That would have been a great idea if the toilet seat wasn't plastic and already cracked down the middle. Her foot went right through. She fell over and somehow broke her hip in the process. On top of all that, she's old. So I'll have to help her through a surgery, some physical therapy, and household chores for the next few months. Of course, the first chore on the list she is already compiling, with great delight I might add, is to..."

"Fix the toilet seat," Norah said laughing as she finished his sentence.

"You got it!" He said with a tired smile. "So, that's why I'm late," he explained as he stepped up on the treadmill. Norah began to collect her things as she prepared to leave.

"Well, I guess I'll see you next time," Norah commented with apparent disappointment in her voice.

"Oh, by the way, did you and your hubby get a chance to meet the tele-evangelist?"

Putting her hand on her hip and with a slight shake of her head, she answered playfully, "We sure did. And before you even ask, he did not pass an offering plate or ask us for any money."

"Will you see him again?"

"Yeah. Why?"

"Ask him to pray for my mother, Rose. She really has a long road ahead."

"Will do. See you later." She put her gym bag over her shoulder and headed out. The amazing thing though is that her gym bag wasn't nearly as heavy as the guilt she was carrying.

Walking through the front door of her home, she caught a glimpse of a book on the coffee table. She hung her keys on the nail on the wall that she had put there out of frustration one day because she kept losing her keys. As she went to see what book it was, she heard Owen flushing the hallway toilet. "Is that a Bible?" she thought to herself trying to look as if she were not interested.

"I'm fixing to get in the bed," Owen said to the passerby in his own home.

With a shrug of her shoulders she went directly into the master bathroom and closed the door. Owen, on the other hand, pulled down the covers of the bed and climbed under with a prayer, "God help us."

Her mind was racing as she got ready for the shower. "Who does he think he is?" She began to question. She could feel the smirk on her face as she continued to think, "He can't just throw a Bible out on the table and expect me to think he is some holy man, some Billy Graham, some Paul the Apostle."

She walked into her closet to get dressed for bed. She grabbed a sweatshirt from the right side and a pair of sweat pants from the left side. While putting in her left leg, she thought of Pastor Schaeffer's drawing. She could see the arrow under her stick figure pointing away from Owen. To top it all off, she became angry because she couldn't shake the imagery of the two closets from her mind. As she pulled up her sweatpants, the question scrolled across her mind like a marquis, "Are those old-closet clothes or new- closet clothes?"

She was so heavily laden with guilt over her actions and burdened down with Pastor Schaeffer's drawings and analogies, that she walked right pass the king size bed and headed into the living room. She sat down in the recliner and turned on the television. All the while, she constrained her eyes from looking at the Bible, and resisted all temptation to pick it up. "This is probably some sick test Owen has put together. More than likely he has the Bible at some perfect angle. If I move it, he will know it." She ignored the Bible and fell asleep in the chair for most of the night.

Around four in the morning she woke up and headed toward the king sized bed. She had a kink in her neck and was thankful to get out of the chair. As her head hit the pillow, Owen woke up. His eyes adjusted to see the time and then closed. He went fast asleep.

CHAPTER FIVE

"So let's talk about quality time," Pastor Schaeffer opened their session with a serious look on his face. He had been running all day long and knew if he sat too still he might fall asleep. He rocked back and forth in his office chair and sipped his coffee to stay energized.

"Pastor, we honestly don't spend any time together anymore. Mostly it is my fault, I have to admit." Pastor Schaeffer was almost taken back by Owen's transparency. Norah, on the other hand, was disgusted; of course she didn't let it show. All she did the first five or ten minutes of the session was sit quietly.

"Norah, what about you? How would you say your time is spent in relation to Owen? Would you say you are distant from him?" Pastor asked this leading question on purpose. He knew isolation was a major factor in the red marriage and needed to be discussed.

"I suppose I am distant. I usually do my thing and he does his."

Looking at his notes, Pastor Schaeffer asked a very strong question, "Are you still spending time with Allen?"

"Like I said last time," Norah justified, "I have made no appointments with him. However, I do have a friend whose mom isn't doing well. Please keep her in your prayers."

"Norah, you are pulling away from your marriage. You are isolating yourself," Pastor explained and then turned to Owen, "And you are really doing the same thing." Taking a deep breath he took his Bible off the bookshelf behind him and laid it on his desk. He opened to Proverbs 18:1. Turning the Bible around to face Norah he asked her to read the highlighted verse:

He who isolates himself seeks his own desire, he quarrels against all sounds wisdom.—Proverbs 18:1

Pastor Schaeffer used his fingers to count off the major points of a marriage in the red. "So what have we learned about the red? It is characterized by invisible walls, by independent lives, and by isolation. A tempting resolution for isolation is divorce. Tell me this: how often have you guys talked about divorce?"

"Too many times to count." Owen said looking at Norah who was affirming his answer by nodding her head.

"You remember the story of Jonah, right?"

"Yes," they both replied.

"Well, before Jonah was ever swallowed by a big fish, he chose to be disobedient to God. His rebellion can be easily identified by his isolation. Scripture shows that Jonah took the route opposite to the one God told him to take, and he always went down." He then shared the direction of Jonah's life by emphasizing the word "down". "His isolation took him "down": down to Joppa, down to Tarshish, down into the hull of the ship, down into the water, and finally, down into the belly of a fish."

"So what does Jonah's going down have to do with our marriage?" Norah asked as she furrowed her brow.

Placing his coffee on an aged, dilapidated coaster which read, "#1 Dad," Pastor Schaeffer leaned up in his chair and said, "Listen, before you live a life isolated from your spouse, you first choose to live isolated from God. Isolation from God always takes a person down."

The statement pierced Owen's heart. He remembered a time when he was growing in his faith. In fact, he could still picture the waves crashing late one evening as he walked along the shore. It was the final night of a student camp prior to his high school graduation and new life in college. He had experienced God in a fresh way. On that evening he remembered walking and talking with God and hoped he would never take his eyes off Christ. However, Pastor's statement about isolation was true. Somewhere, somehow, someday--Owen began to drift.

"I also want you to know," Pastor continued, "isolation is a by-product of demonic oppression." Norah didn't flinch on the first statement, but this one got her attention.

"Good grief, Pastor! I came here to get some help, not to be slandered! I know we have some problems, but demon possession? That's a little much, don't you think?" All she could picture in her mind was that horrible movie her cousin talked her into watching when she was little, *The Exorcist*. Since that time whenever she heard the phrase "demon possession", she always pictured that little girl's head spinning around.

"I did not say you were *possessed*." Pastor Schaeffer explained further, speaking slowly his next sentence, "I said you were *oppressed*. Let me explain. You are not inhabited by a demon, but you are being pushed around." He took his Bible and turned it back toward him while flipping to the book of Mark. "In Mark 5 we read an account of demonic possession which always gets my attention." He began to read the verses aloud:

When He [Jesus] got out of the boat and immediately a man from the tombs with an unclean spirit met him, and he had his dwelling among the tombs. And no one was able to bind him anymore, even with a chain...(vs 5) Constantly night and day, he was screaming among the tombs in the mountains and gashing himself with stones.—Mark 5:1-2, 5

After hearing the verses, Owen asked inquisitively, "So what does this teach us?"

"Well, a couple of interesting things here about the demon possessed man. First, he isolated himself and lived an unclean life. Tombs were considered unclean according to Jewish belief. This man made his home there. Secondly, it is obvious the man found no satisfaction in his life of isolation. He was depressed, evidenced by his screaming and cutting himself."

"Pastor, you said this man was possessed, but we are merely oppressed. So how does this have anything to do with us?" Norah asked with a sense of impatience in her voice.

"It applies, I believe, because as I counsel couples in the red, I see them pulling away from God and their spouse. That is the isolation. They begin to hang out in the tombs so to speak. In your case, with Allen. However, I have never found anyone who found satisfaction, happiness, or whatever they were looking for in an ungodly life."

Norah sat there shell shocked. She was stunned that Pastor would just point out her sin so openly. In fact, she began to think he was judgmental and perhaps believed himself to be "Mr. High and Mighty" without any problems. Her thoughts were interrupted by the Pastor's words which made Norah think he was a mind reader.

"Norah, I'm not trying to be judgmental or act all "high and mighty" here. If I didn't care about your relationship with Jesus and Owen, I would never have been so blunt." Giving Norah some time to think and the Holy Spirit an opportunity to work on her, Pastor Schaeffer turned his attention to Owen.

"Owen, you isolated yourself at home and then began to surf the web for pornography. That is hanging out in the tombs. Have you done anything about that, by the way?" Pastor Schaeffer noticed a difference in Owen's demeanor, but wasn't completely sure what was going on.

Owen slid up on the edge of his seat preparing to give his answer. He wanted to be sensitive, however, to Norah. He didn't want to give her the impression that he was the "angel" of the two, because he was not.

"Pastor, when we were with you last time I felt like a failure. I was filthy dirty with sin. I not only was hanging out in the tombs, I was practically dead. Like the possessed man you just spoke about: I was miserable." He looked at the floor as if to remember the past embarrassment of his actions.

"When we left your office last week, I drove straight to Wal-Mart and I picked up some software. Norah put a password on it, and I haven't looked at anything inappropriate for seven days. I also got my Bible out and began to read a little." He stopped there, even though he wanted to share more. He really sensed he was walking and talking with God again, not as close as his early college years, but much closer than in recent months.

The Holy Spirit was working on Norah as she sat in her chair. She knew she had made no steps to help the marriage in the past week. She was angry and even a bit jealous of Owen because of his progress and sad at her apathy. She blurted out before she had time to think, "Okay, I'll stop going to the gym where Allen is!"

Her remark came out of nowhere and took both Owen and Pastor Schaeffer by surprise. Owen leaned back in his seat while Pastor began, "Norah, its time for you to get out of the tombs. As a follower of Christ you will never be satisfied in sin. I am proud of you. I am praying for you, both of you."

Pastor Schaeffer then stood up and turned to look at his book shelf. Owen got a bit nervous because he had heard Pastor loved to give books out for people to read, but he hated reading. If he were going to pull down a book, Owen prayed for a thin one with a huge font. Much to his surprise, Pastor Schaeffer reached up and grabbed a small red wooden box on his shelf. He took the box and put it in the center of his desk and then asked, "Would you like to get out of the red?"

Owen answered quickly, "That's why we are here."

CHAPTER SIX

N orah felt the box was a bit hokey, but she was extremely curious about what might be in it. Owen, on the other hand, sat back up in his chair and leaned in.

"Nothing's going to jump out of the box, is it?" Norah asked with a smile on her face.

Pastor Schaeffer paused immediately and looked at her deadly seriously, "I need to warn you, Norah, last time I opened this box, the wife fainted." He then began to reach for the box.

With her eyes bugging out of her head she jumped out of her seat, blocked Schaeffer's hand from opening the box, and said, "Wait!"

Pastor Schaeffer threw his head back and began laughing uncontrollably. "Norah, I'm just kidding." He then opened the lid to the box and shouted, "Boo!" He continued to laugh.

"Good one, Pastor," Owen said while laughing at Norah.

"That is not funny," Norah said sitting back down in her chair with a smile on her face.

"The box is where I keep the cards needed to help marriages in the red. In fact, I actually open this box about once a month. Believe it or not, you aren't the only ones whose marriage is in the red."

Opening the box, he pulled out a stack of cards which had a red border. The stack was separated by paper clips into three smaller stacks. He pulled two cards out of each stack. It was apparent that both Norah and Owen would be given a set of these cards.

Still in a joking mood, Owen said, "So what's the lowest bet on this card game?"

Even Norah chimed in, "All I have is a hundred." Norah and Owen shared a smile. Norah quickly wiped the smile off her face and looked at the floor. It felt awkward joking with Owen again; it had been so long.

"I can't play cards with you! I lost all my money last night," Pastor Schaeffer replied laughing again. Owen was kind of impressed with Pastor's sense of humor. He assumed all preachers were dull and dry because he thought most preachers were dull and dry in the pulpit.

"You both get a set of these cards. Let me give you one card at a time so I can explain." He dealt the cards to them. "The first card gives a list of your morning prayer goals. You need to put this card where you will certainly see it. You can use these cards as book marks in your Bible, put them on the mirror where you get ready in the morning, or I have known some to put them on the speed-o-meter of their cars."

Norah and Owen both glanced over the card. There were three bullet point statements written in 18 font and double spaced. Pastor Schaeffer sat back in his seat and prepared to explain the prayer goals.

"Let's do this with audience participation." Pastor Schaeffer said. "Owen, since you are designed by God to be the spiritual leader of the family, why don't you read the first statement?"

"No problem." He read the statement out loud. "I must choose to change today."

Pastor Schaeffer pointed out, "Remember the closets?" They both nodded their heads. "Oftentimes in marriage the wife spends her time trying to fix the husband while the husband tries to fix the wife. That is completely backward. Norah, you can't change Owen. Owen, you can't change Norah."

He continued while opening his Bible to 1 Timothy 4:7b, "Paul wrote to young Timothy a word of encouragement:"

Discipline yourself for the purpose of godliness.—
1 Timothy 4:7b

"The word used here by Paul for discipline is a Greek word which gives us our English word, gymnasium. Paul was letting Timothy know that godliness was attained through personal discipline. Just like exercising."

"Norah," he continued his mini-sermon looking toward her, "you are very disciplined in exercising. In the same way you are disciplined in that area of your life, you must choose to be disciplined in the area of godliness. Therefore, you have to begin your prayer life by saying, 'Lord, today I choose to change myself. I need Your help to make that happen.' Make sense?"

Norah looked at Pastor Schaeffer and said, "Makes sense to me."

"Owen, I want to make this plain to both of you. On your own, without the help of God, the Holy Spirit within you, there will be no life change. Although you have purchased the software for your computer and done well for the past week, you will still continue to struggle. There is no doubt in my mind, pornography has tainted your view of all women. You probably look at women as sexual objects now instead of people. Well, that is sin."

"You are going to have to learn to fight against that. The real battle, however, is with yourself: your flesh, your old life, your old sin nature. So you must choose to crucify--put to death--sinful thoughts and attitudes. You have to remind yourself that you are dead to sin. Paul wrote in Galatians 2:20:

I have been crucified with Christ; and it is no longer I who live, but Christ lives in me; and the life which I now live in the flesh I live by faith in the Son of God, who loved me and gave himself up for me.—Galatians 2:20

"Through prayer and use of the Word of God, the Sword of the Holy Spirit, you have to put to death every thought, attitude or action which is sinful. A simple question you can ask yourself each morning is, 'What sins will I need to put to death today?' "

"Let's face it," Pastor continued, "We typically know everyday what areas are going to consume us. So we have to be prepared. Norah, when you begin thinking about going to the gym to hang out with Allen, you have to mortify or put to death that fleshly action through prayer and scripture."

Owen and Norah had never heard such graphic language about sin. Put it to death; mortify it. The concept definitely would stick.

"You know, I have found it helpful to write in my journal the top ten temptations of my life which I need to be certain to kill on the spot. I then just pray through them. For example, I might pray, 'Today, Lord, I know I will be tempted to lust after a woman. I pray now You would bring to mind Galatians 2:20 when the temptation arises. I choose to crucify that sin.'"

Owen thought to himself, "Pastor struggles with lust?"

Much to Owen's surprise, Pastor said, "I know you are shocked that a Pastor would be tempted to lust. But let's get real. I face the same temptations as everyone else. I fight the same dragons everyone else does. I'm not exempt from temptation just because I am a preacher. I wish that were the case; it would make preaching a lot easier, I think. Norah, why don't you read number two?"

Looking down at her card still thinking about what Pastor Schaeffer just said, she appreciated her Pastor's transparency . . . it offered her hope. She read slowly, "I must fight the real enemy today."

"Owen, this is easily said, but not easily done. The number one priority of our life must be our relationship with Jesus. Second to that is our relationship with our spouse. Now I know this may shock both of you, but I want you to look at one another face to face." Norah and Owen reluctantly turned toward one another, both strangely curious about what would come next. You never know with Pastor Schaeffer.

"Norah, you see Owen?" She didn't answer, assuming it was merely a rhetorical question. He continued anyway, "Owen is not your problem. Owen is not your enemy."

"Now, Owen, you see Norah? She is not your problem. She is not your enemy."

This idea really had never dawned on either of them. The assumption is that within marriage problems, the problem is the spouse. As they were still looking at one another, they could hear Pastor Schaeffer turning pages in his Bible. Norah turned her head confident they didn't need to look at one another anymore.

"Look back at each other," Pastor Schaeffer said, "Listen to this Scripture Paul wrote in the book of Ephesians 6:12:

For our struggle is not against flesh and blood, but against rulers, against the powers, against the world forces of this darkness, against the spiritual forces of wickedness in heavenly places.—Ephesians 6:12

"Now, I want you to squeeze one another's cheeks." They both turned to and looked at him, sure this was another joke.

"You want me to squeeze her cheek?" Owen asked. "Is there a point to this?"

"I not only want you to squeeze her cheek, I want her to squeeze yours." Neither of them budged. "The quicker you do this, the quicker I can make the point." They reluctantly gave in.

Norah grabbed a hunk of Owen's cheek first. She got a good grip, too; the entire side of his face stretched out like a piece of taffy. Not to be outdone, Owen reached over with two hands and grabbed two handfuls of skin.

"Go easy on her," Pastor Schaeffer said with a quiet, but noticeable chuckle. "Tell me, Norah, is Owen made of flesh and blood?"

"Of course," she said with a little drool coming out of the side of his mouth. He couldn't control it because of the tight pulling of his cheek.

"Gross!" She said as she let go of his cheek, wiping the slobber off her hand.

"Owen, what about you? Do you feel flesh?"

"Sure do," he let go revealing two large red spots which quickly disappeared on each side of her face. Thankfully, too. Pastor tried to imagine explaining a counseling session in which the wife looked as if she had been slapped.

"Here's the point." They both looked at him. "Your wrestling and fighting with one another keeps you stagnant and unproductive, wasting your energy. You are not fighting the real enemy. Your real enemy is the devil. He desires to split up the marriage; that's his number one goal. He's good at it, too. Unless you choose to fight the real enemy, you will keep on fighting one another. Spiritual warfare happens in the realm of relationships. The enemy wants to disrupt every relationship of our lives. Few things bring him more joy than to see husbands and wives fighting one another. One of his highest priorities is to destroy the sacred union of marriage."

"That's a good point. But why did you make us squeeze one another's face?" Norah asked.

"Because you will never forget the point now, will you? So let's recap quickly. Each morning you need to pray to God, 'Lord, I choose to change today. Help me.' Secondly, you can pray, 'Lord,

I choose to fight the real enemy. Help me.'" Pointing at Owen, he said, "Go ahead and read number three."

Owen, rubbing his check, read the final statement on the card, "I must choose to value my marriage today."

"No one else will value your marriage for you. You have to choose daily to consider your marriage valuable. People whose marriages are in the red don't usually value their marriage at all. So you have to pray and ask the Lord to enable you to consider your marriage of great worth."

Again Pastor Schaeffer flipped to another verse in his Bible. Owen was disappointed that he hadn't written down the previous verses so he could look them up later; he desired to memorize them. He had gotten 1 John 1:9 down; that's for sure.

Schaeffer shared another verse; "Hebrews 13:4 makes this statement:"

Marriage is to be held in honor among all and the marriage bed is to be undefiled; for fornicators and adulterers God will punish.—Hebrews 13:4

The bite of conviction sank deeply into Norah's conscience. Although she hadn't committed adultery, she was definitely attaching herself emotionally to Allen. She was one step away from a moral nose dive. There was no doubt that she was dishonoring her marriage. Her actions revealed that truth. However, she resolved to make a change.

"Okay, okay," Norah began to speak up as her eyes filled with tears, "I have to ask the Lord to forgive me. I will stop going to exercise…" she paused and then honestly confessed, "…going to meet Allen." Up until this point Norah seemed to be hard as a rock.

Pastor Schaeffer prayed silently, "Thank You, Lord. Your Word is like a hammer which breaks the hard heart. Thank You, thank You for penetrating Norah's heart with Your Word. Continue to work."

Owen reached over and grabbed Norah's hand. Interlocking their fingers, they squeezed tightly. "I forgive you. Forgive me?" Owen asked with great sadness over his sin. He wished he hadn't ever gotten caught up in his pornography.

"Of course."

Owen then looked at Pastor Schaeffer and questioned him, "Do you think you can write down those three verses you just read to us? I think they would be a huge help."

Pastor Schaeffer dealt the second card in the three-card deck. This card had all three verses written on it. "Throughout the day you will want to keep this card with you. Memorize these verses. The Scripture will help keep you focused on getting out of the red."

After taking the second card and glancing at it, Norah and Owen received the third card. "Now this card has three questions on it that you will need to ask yourselves at the end of the day. If you fail to assess your progress at the end of each day, you will stunt your growth in the recovery process.

Pastor Schaeffer designed the third card with the same red border as the others to motivate dependence upon God for change. The questions had an obvious correlation to the three prayer goals and the three verses.

- What attitudes and actions have I crucified today?
- Have I identified and fought the real enemy today?
- How have I shown my spouse that I value our marriage today?

After a short discussion of the questions, Norah inquired, "So how long do we do this?"

"Let's put you on these cards for a couple of weeks. I spoke with Addison last night about having you over for dinner two weeks from today. How does that sound?"

"Deal. Do you need me to bring anything?" Norah asked.

"No. Don't worry about it. My wife loves to cook. You just bring your cards."

"When do we start on the yellow marriage?" Owen asked.

"We'll see. Let me pray for you before you leave."

PART II:

MARRIAGE IN THE YELLOW

"What attitudes and actions have I crucified today?" Owen read audibly as he sat at the kitchen table that evening just before bed. Norah was reading the same list of questions while in bed. She had positioned the pillows on the headboard for comfort and looked intently at the cards given to her by Pastor Schaeffer.

After they left Pastor Schaeffer's office last week, they both decided to purchase a journal. They "pinky promised" one another, like they did when they first started dating, that they would write their thoughts and prayers in a journal. Norah picked out a journal which had a picture of flowers on the front of it. Owen, not wanting to look like a sissy, found a journal made of genuine leather. He was willing to pay extra just so it wouldn't look effeminate. Norah was committed to the process of writing, but Owen was a bit unpredictable. Some days he really enjoyed writing; other days, however, not so much.

Sitting at the kitchen table with a bowl of Moose Tracks Ice Cream, Owen was on a writing streak. In fact, this particular night he couldn't write fast enough:

I was highly tempted today as I worked on my computer. As I was checking my e-mail I found two e-mails which seemed to audibly call out my name. The subject line of both familiarly read: XXX Open Me. The first thing I did was look around to see if anyone was watching. This overwhelming "thing" rose up inside of me which had an insatiable desire to open the e-mail. This thing began to take control. I could even sense darkness closing in all around me. It was thick in the room. I grabbed the mouse and ran the little arrow over the e-mail which promised pleasure and fulfillment...

The e-mails weren't unusual at all. Owen used to open them practically every time he checked his e-mail. The first time he opened an e-mail like this, he remembered the throbbing ache of conviction in his heart. However, the loud conviction he once heard developed into a faint whisper. Over time he had learned to ignore it completely.

Owen could remember one of the illustrations Pastor Schaeffer used last Sunday morning as he preached on the conviction of the Holy Spirit. "How many of you press *snooze* on your alarm clock?" Pastor Schaeffer asked the congregation. About eighty percent of the people in the small crowd raised their hands while everyone snickered a little bit. "All right, let me ask you another question. How many of you have hit the snooze button so many times that you finally just began to sleep right through the alarm?" Just about everyone began to laugh aloud because they identified with the concept of sleeping through the alarm.

Pastor Schaeffer had a way of getting everyone laughing, and then he would slip in a profound Biblical truth. "I want you to know that the Holy Spirit sounds an alarm in your heart when you are tempted to sin and during the act of the sin. His conviction warns you to wake up and see that you are close to surrendering to the wrong choice. However, the problem is that we often hit the snooze button on the alarm, don't we? The more you hit the snooze button on the alarming conviction of the Holy Spirit in your life, the easier it will be to sleep through it as you sin. Stop hitting the snooze button on the alarm of conviction! Wake up and choose to be holy."

Owen continued in his journal:

While everything around me seemed dark, there was an alarm going off in my heart. The Holy Spirit was convicting me of my actions. He then brought to mind part of my memory verse for the week: I have been crucified with Christ. That simple phrase grew louder and louder in my soul. And like light dispels the darkness, the Scripture pushed away that evil desire in me and I checked "delete" on both e-mails. So what actions have I crucified today? I put to death the desire to look at something which would have destroyed my view of Norah. I crucified my flesh! Thank You, Jesus, for Your help.

Owen took a huge bite of his Moose Tracks and did a mini celebration dance in his chair. Just down the hall beneath the dim light of the bedroom lamp Norah sat. Owen's victory was a quick one; however, Norah was still fighting ferociously. She had not been to the gym for three days. In fact, she rarely even thought about Allen. He had been pushed into the basement of her mind. Her major problem was Owen.

She could not shake the image of him sitting in front of the computer gawking at naked women all evening long. Her entire self-image was attacked all day. She couldn't walk past a mirror without conducting a horrible examination of herself. Grabbing a small roll of fat on her side she thought to herself, "No wonder he looks at that stuff. I am a total mess." Sitting in the bed that evening in a night gown, which she swore she would never wear, she thought to herself, "Why would he even want to come to bed with me?"

She was so frustrated with herself and Owen that she could barely look at him throughout the day. She held a disgust toward him which seemed to grow stronger and even wanted to come out in anger. Norah's arsenal was fully loaded with smart-aleck ammunition, ready to gun down any comment made by Owen. For example, Owen actually made a positive comment at supper, "This meal looks great." All Norah could think as she slung a helping on his plate was, "As great as all those women?!" Owen realized her anger but chose to keep silent.

She held her red daily questions card in front of her and read audibly, "Have I identified and fought the real enemy today?" Putting the card down with her mind racing, she began to write in her journal:

> God, I need You to help me fight the real enemy. I know the devil desires to destroy my relationship with Owen. I also know, God, that I must learn to forgive. But, Lord, I feel so ugly. I feel like I must really be gross to look at, or Owen would have eyes only for me. God, what is wrong with me? Lord, maybe I am being over sensitive, over critical, or over something; I don't know. I do know that I desperately need your help. Help me to fight the real enemy tomorrow. Help my attitude toward Owen to be completely changed.

About that time she heard Owen's ice cream bowl hit the sink in the kitchen. Tossing his bowl into the sink was typically the last thing he would do before heading off to bed. She quickly put up her journal and Scripture memory cards and turned out the light. She pulled the covers up and was completely still when Owen opened the bedroom door. "Norah," Owen whispered, "You awake?"

She chose not to respond to his question for fear it might lead to intimacy. Norah wasn't in the mood for any of that, so she pretended to be asleep. Owen went into the master bathroom, brushed his teeth, and quietly went to bed. Climbing under the covers, Owen was out like a light. Norah laid there in the darkness for two hours before she finally fell asleep.

CHAPTER TWO

He rolled over and pressed the alarm clock, another reminder of Pastor's message on Sunday. He turned over to see if Norah was asleep. However, Norah wasn't in the bed. He adjusted his eyes to the dark room and realized she was already up. "What is she doing up at 6:30 in the morning?" he thought.

Just about that time he heard footsteps down the hall. There was one unavoidable board, just beneath the carpet, which always creaked when you stepped on it. The floor made that guaranteed sound, indicating Norah's soon arrival. What Owen was about to see would certainly shock him.

She had a tray in her hands which was filled with all of Owen's favorites. "Good morning," she said laying the tray down on the bed. Flipping on the lamp, Owen was astonished and taken back by what he saw. She hadn't fixed him breakfast in bed. . . *ever*. This was a first. There was coffee, orange juice, a stack of pancakes, scrambled eggs, two pieces of bacon and buttered toast.

"What is all of this?" Owen questioned with obvious confusion.

"It's breakfast, of course," Norah replied, "I just want you to know that I love you."

It had been some time since Owen had heard Norah make that comment. "Norah, I love you, too."

At about that time a voice echoed down the hallway, "Mommy! Mommy!" Norah stood up rolled her eyes and walked out of their bedroom. She chose to tend to the children so Owen could enjoy a peaceful breakfast. Owen wasn't a huge breakfast eater, but he sat in the bed and ate every bite. The only thing left on the plate was a small puddle of syrup left over from the pancakes.

"Thanks for the breakfast! That really meant a lot." Owen said looking into Norah's eyes as he finished tying his tie. "I may be late tonight; we are trying to finish up the project I was telling you about that's due next week. We will probably just order Chinese for supper and eat in the office."

Running late became the evening trend for the next five nights. Norah was overwhelmingly frustrated by his lack of time at home with her and the children. However, she didn't say a word to him. She kept quiet and stuck to her red cards. "His off day will be different," she confidently thought to herself. She could leave the children with him for a couple of hours while she did some grocery shopping, and then they could hang out together all afternoon.

Norah was checking her e-mail when she noticed a message from Owen. She hardly ever got an e-mail from Owen and was looking forward to reading what he had written. Filled with anticipation she began to read:

```
I hope your day is going well. We just
finished up the project and the manager
loved it. He gave Jim and me a free round
of golf at the Gates Country Club. Jim
and I have decided to take our off day
tomorrow and hit the links! Just letting
you know our tee time is at 8 a.m. We
```

should be done sometime after lunch
around 2. Don't wait up tonight. We have
a few loose ends we have to tie up for
the big corporate presentation first of
next week.

Like a balloon with a slow and steady leak, Norah's anticipation had drastically deflated with every line she read in the e-mail. Instinctively anger began to present itself. Then she began to tear up. "What is his problem?" She thought to herself. "I have been slaving in this house all week long. I can't go shopping for groceries with the children. It's a total nightmare trying to do that! I have been wiping runny noses all week long, changing diapers, feeding screaming kids and the one small break at the grocery store I was looking forward to has been taken away from me!"

The vibration of her cell phone interrupted her thoughts. It was a short vibration which ended with a single beep, indicating that she had a text message. Norah reached over to get her phone which was charging on the nightstand. She clicked on the text message, "Where have you been? I have been hitting the treadmill all by myself for a week!"

Her heart skipped a beat; Allen, who had been in the basement of her mind, suddenly jumped into the foyer. "What do I do?" she thought. "Do I text him back? Should I respond to him?" Norah heard a scream coming from the living room and jumped to her feet to find out it's source. "I'll deal with this later," she said quietly as she put the phone down next to the computer.

Breaking up the children's fight over a broken crayon, she kept thinking about Allen's text. Not only was his text message on her mind, but so was Owen's e-mail. You have one guy, Allen, who seemed to want to spend time with Norah. You have another guy, Owen, who seemed to care less about spending time with her. She struggled with what to do all afternoon and into the evening.

After the children's baths Norah put them into their beds. Owen was still at work. Norah was exhausted as she sat down on the couch. She then heard another beep from the phone. With renewed energy she went to pick it up. All the while she was hoping it was Allen sending her another message. She opened up the text message and, much to her delight, it was him, "Will you be here tonight?"

Norah sat down pondering how to answer his question. About that time another text landed on her phone, "I really miss seeing you." She now felt pressured to answer. Logic coaxed her into the temptation to communicate with him; not returning his text would be rude.

Although she hated trying to type a message on her cell phone, Norah answered his question. "Sorry not there. Been very busy 2. Not there tonight. I miss you 2." Before pressing *send* on her cell phone and delivering her message to Allen in a millisecond, she reread her message about four times. She finally decided to erase the last line before she pressed *send*.

Moments later on her cell phone was a another text, nothing but a colon and an opening parenthesis sign, ":(" representing his disappointment.. Norah gave no response. She erased her text messages and plugged her phone back into the charger.

"Two more days and we eat with Pastor Schaeffer and his wife. I hope and pray he doesn't ask me about Allen," Norah reflected as she went off to sleep. Norah's heart ached to be desired.

Owen came in late that night and climbed into bed next to Norah, who was sound asleep. The next morning came quickly. Owen took off from the house to hit the links.

"Are you going to get that?" Owen screamed from a scalding hot shower as the phone rang. Norah was steaming after being with the kids all day long waiting for Owen to get in from his precious round of golf. He said he would be home at two o' clock. It was 3:45 p.m. and he just haphazardly walked through the door. All he said was, "I am dog-tired. I'm going to take a quick shower and then a little nap before supper."

"You get it! I am trying to get the kids ready so we can go grocery shopping." She responded with obvious gravel in her voice. She was so angry she couldn't see straight. She couldn't believe Owen didn't volunteer to keep the children.

Owen jumped out of the shower and ran to the phone. He normally would ignore the ring, but he was expecting a call from his manager. They were going to set the time when they would make their presentation to Corporate. Soaking wet with a towel draped around him, he grabbed the phone, "Hello, this is Owen."

"Owen, how's it going?"

Owen didn't recognize the voice. He hated it when people assumed he knew who it was on the other end of the line. "It's going well."

"Are you coming out of the red?" Owen was stunned, immediately recognizing Pastor Schaeffer's voice.

Gaining his composure after being mugged by reality he responded, "We are doing much better, Pastor. Thanks."

"Well, I was just calling to remind you about our supper tomorrow night. Addison is preparing some homemade bread right now. You should smell it. You are going to be impressed with my wife's cooking. How does six o' clock sound?"

"That sounds great, Pastor! Norah and I were just talking about how excited we are about hanging out with you." He lied. "Will see you tomorrow night. I have the GPS already set with your address in it," he lied again.

"Sounds great. We look forward to seeing you tomorrow," Pastor Schaeffer said as he hung up the phone.

"Who was that?" Norah screamed down the hall.

"Pastor Schaeffer. He was just reminding us about tomorrow night. Honey, do you think you could grab me some more deodorant at the grocery store? I am just about out," he said as he jumped back into the shower.

Norah didn't reply. She just put the children in the van and took off. "Get him some deodorant. I'd like to get him some deodorant and shove it down his throat," she thought to herself. "I can't believe he is so inconsiderate."

CHAPTER THREE

They stood on a mat which read, "Welcome," after ringing the doorbell to Pastor Schaeffer's home. They both were nervous. Even though Norah had grown up in church, she had never been invited to eat at the Pastor's house. Owen wasn't sure how it would be either. He felt like he was about to enter one of those fancy restaurants where he didn't know which fork he was supposed to use. Pastor Schaeffer swung the door open and said, "Hello! Welcome! How are you doing?"

He extended a half-hug to Norah and shook Owen's hand. "Come on in. Addison just took the pizza out of the box." He said it loud enough for Addison to hear in the kitchen.

"Schaeffer, you know good and well I didn't order a pizza," she said as she entered the foyer with a sideways glance at Schaeffer and her hands on her hips. "How are you both doing, Norah and Owen? I have heard so much about you." She went straight to Norah and gave her a great big hug.

"You have a beautiful home, Mrs. Addison."

"Mrs. Addison! You just call me Addi. I am only about five years older than you, girl." She said with a high pitched giggle. "Now

Owen," she said reaching out her right hand to shake his, "you need to call me Mrs. Addison." Pulling him in she gave him and hug and said, "You know I'm just kidding."

They all laughed together as Pastor Schaeffer led them into the kitchen, which showed the evidence of Addi's preparation. Norah was shocked with the "normal" décor in their home. She expected a bunch of angel statues, crucifixes, paintings of Jesus, and praying hands. As they entered the kitchen, Nora was surprised to see that Addison's arrangement on her table was the same as the one she had at home.

"I have that same arrangement at home," Norah said, pointing at the flowers.

"You know, I found that at T.J. Maxx the other day and couldn't pass it up."

"That is so funny. I found mine at Marshalls about a month ago."

Addi went on to explain, "I am a huge fan of Marshalls and T.J. Maxx. I have always said there is no use paying full price when you can just wait a month and get it for less."

Schaeffer took the arrangement off the table and said, "I am just going to remove this bush from the table so we can see one another while we are eating."

"We have pork chops, green beans, rice with tomato gravy, and sweet corn for tonight. I hope you brought your appetite, Owen." Addi happily announced as she fixed each plate and passed it on to Schaeffer to put on the table.

"Just go ahead and grab a seat anywhere you like. What would you like to drink? We have tea and water."

Norah said, "Water will be fine."

"I'll take some tea, please." Owen responded.

After blessing the food, Schaeffer opened up the subject of their marriage. "I have let Addi know your marriage is in the red. She knows exactly what that means because she has seen so many in the red. So, let's talk. How are you doing? Owen, we will start with you."

Since they knew Addison would be part of the counseling, they weren't surprised she had been given the full story. "She and I have been doing much better over the past two weeks. In fact, when we left your office, we went to the local bookstore and picked up two journals. This gave us the opportunity to write what God was teaching us concerning our red cards." He paused for just a moment to get a drink of tea, "Now I'm not going to lie to you. I haven't written in my journal every single day, nor have I read every card each day. But I have done it about ninety percent of the time." He cut into his pork chop and took a bite, looking at Norah.

"I have written in my journal every single day. I have all the verses memorized, and they have really helped. But I will have to disagree with Owen on how we are doing." It felt good to have her feelings out in the open.

Owen quickly snapped his head toward Norah and said, "What are you talking about? We haven't been yelling at each other. I haven't been on the internet. I thought things were going well."

"Typical male," Addi said looking at Owen. "It's not your fault. You probably just haven't picked up on what most women view as problems. Oftentimes we have to train our men," she said with a little laugh as she looked at Schaeffer.

"You got that right. She has trained me well," Schaeffer grinned, looking over the table at Owen. "You'll figure it out. It just takes some time." Shifting his undivided attention to Norah, he asked, "So, why would you say these past couple of weeks weren't so good?"

"Well, from a positive standpoint I will say that Owen has begun to communicate a little more with me. And there is no doubt the invisible walls which have been built are on their way down."

"That's good. So what has been the issue?" Schaeffer asked.

"Yeah, tell us what has been the issue?" Owen asked sarcastically while stuffing his mouth with green beans and pointing his fork at Norah. Owen was shocked that there might still be a problem and was embarrassed in front of Addison.

"Let me remind you, Owen," Schaeffer replied in a serious manner, "if you take a sarcastic tone in our talks together, Norah will never feel free to actually open up. So pay close attention to not only *what* you say but *how* you say it."

Owen's face began to turn red as he wiped the scowl away. "You're right. I'm sorry."

"Don't tell *me*," Schaeffer replied looking intently at Norah, "Tell *her*."

"I'm sorry. Seriously, I shouldn't have made such a dumb comment." Owen seemed sincere enough for Norah to open up.

"Well, the first few days after we left your office, things were great. But you know, then life started happening. Owen had a huge project at work he had to tend to. He spent nine out of fourteen nights working late. I really sought to give him the benefit of the doubt. But then, on his off day, he and a buddy of his spent eight hours on the golf course. When he got home, did he say, 'Honey, let me help with the kids. You go and do what you need to do?' No. He said, 'I'm going to take a shower and a nap.' So I had to take both kids, kicking and screaming, with me to the grocery store. Needless to say, he didn't consider me at all in any of his choices."

Following this barrage of statements which made Owen's sweet corn begin to taste sour, everyone looked at him. "Okay," he admitted, "I did spend a ton of time at work. But it was the biggest project I have ever been assigned, and if I do well, I might become branch manager. Now as far as golfing goes, just let me explain. Practically every off day I have, Norah gets out of the bed and takes off. She leaves the house for three and sometimes four hours. After I have worked all week long and have one day to sleep in, I am up at the crack of dawn feeding the kids while she's out buying the grocery store and visiting Marshalls. I just figured that I really should have a day off to do what I want to do. So I went golfing."

"You are going to be shocked," Schaeffer said, looking at Addison. "Are you thinking what I'm thinking?"

They simultaneously said, "They are now in the yellow."

Schaeffer stood to his feet and acted for a moment as if he were addressing an entire stadium full of people. "Ladies and Gentlemen," he cleared his throat and took a sip of his water. "This marriage has moved from the red into the yellow. While there are still issues that must be dealt with, we are confident," looking at his wife, "there is a great future in store for this wonderful family, right honey?"

"Amen!" Addison said, clapping her hands. Norah and Owen sat there stunned. They looked like squirrels with packed cheeks in the middle of the road, unsure which way to go as an armored vehicle approached them at blazing speed. "Just relax," Addi said, "he always does this."

The issues which are prevalent for a marriage in the red will always need attention. However, because of the description of their current circumstances, it was obvious to Pastor Schaeffer and Addison that they needed to face the yellow.

He sat back down and said, "Remember, the problem for those in the red is that there were invisible walls, independent lives, and isolation. Well, there are three characteristics of those who are in the yellow, too."

"What are they?" Norah asked.

"I can't tell you all of them in one sitting, but I will tell you the one which is obvious in your marriage. Two words: Inconsistent priorities."

Addison added, "Your priorities are all out of line. Schaeffer and I continually have to check our priorities to make sure we are putting first things first."

"It's really easy," Pastor Schaefer continued, "for me to get my priorities out of line. Our church runs about 250, and sometimes it feels like every one of them wants me for something on the same day. If I'm not careful, I will give my very best effort, passion, energy, and attention to the 250 while ignoring Addison. And you have heard the statement, 'If momma ain't happy, nobody's happy.' Let me assure you, it is true. I think that is found in Proverbs 32." He said laughing. That was obviously a joke that neither Norah nor Owen got because they didn't know Proverbs had only 31 chapters.

"Moving right along," Pastor continued, after realizing his corny joke just went right over both their heads. "Owen, your passion, energy, efforts, and attention are being given at work and not home. Whether this is how you feel or not, Norah views it as if she isn't important to you."

"That's exactly right," Norah agreed. "Sometimes I feel like I get his leftovers. I then start thinking I must not be very important to him or he would make time for me. I start feeling insecure about everything." Owen just hung his head.

"Owen, I know the attention is on you right now, brother, but that's because you are called to be the spiritual leader of the home. It starts with you. But I want you to know I picked up on something during Norah's comments about these past couple of weeks." Schaeffer looked at Norah.

"Norah, it is evident that your priorities are out of line as well. Here is how I know. You are always planning your grocery dates on his off day with out any consideration of his feelings. When you talk about Owen spending time with you, it's rarely just you, but it's the kids, too. In other words you imply, 'He never spends time with the kids and me.'"

Addison nodded her head in agreement and then took over the conversation. "I used to do the same thing to poor Schaeffer. I would take off and leave the kids with him, or I would make him feel guilty for not spending time with the kids and me. Don't get us wrong; it is important to spend time with the kids. Family time is great. But when your priorities are out of line, there is a huge temptation. Schaeffer, tell them what the temptation is."

"Just like in the red, with every characteristic there is a major temptation. The temptation for you both is simply to be selfish." He stood up and walked into the living room. Looking at a shelf full of books, he grabbed a Bible and went back to the table.

"Paul the Apostle wrote a ton of verses about being selfish. In fact, one verse always sticks out to me. He is writing to the church at Philippi. This church had members who were being extremely selfish. As a result there were great divisions among the people. Paul even calls a couple of ladies out by name in chapter four, but that's a whole sermon. Listen to this simple statement:

Do nothing from selfishness or empty conceit, but with humility of mind regard one another as more important than yourselves.--Philippians 2:3

You know your priorities are out of whack when you are making plans and decisions only considering how it will affect you. As a husband, Owen, you can't just make decisions without any consideration of Norah." Pastor Schaeffer took a bite of his pork chop giving Addison an opportunity to speak.

"And, Norah, you can't make plans without considering your husband. You always have to be thinking of his best interest. Also, Owen, you always have to be thinking of her best interest. You are not two people any more. You are one." Addison said with a slight crackle in her voice. It was evident she had learned that lesson the hard way.

After the meal was over, Pastor Schaeffer helped clear the table. They walked to the front door, and Owen asked one last question, "Do we get yellow cards now?"

"Tell you what," Pastor Schaeffer stated. "Let's meet Wednesday afternoon in my office. Just keep the red cards going until then."

CHAPTER FOUR

"Have you ever made a priority list?" Owen asked Norah.

"No, I really haven't. I have thought about it before, but never really made one."

"Okay, well I am always prioritizing work tasks based upon what is most important. So let's think this through for a minute." Owen planned as he sat down on the bed next to Norah that evening. He had a yellow note pad and started off with a simple question, "What should be our number one priority?"

"I know this will sound like a Sunday School answer," Norah said, "but God."

In the top left hand portion of the paper Owen wrote, *God is my number one priority.*

"Am I supposed to read that chicken scratch?" Norah asked jokingly.

"Real funny. Everything *you* write looks like your wrote it with your left foot." They both laughed and Owen continued his priority list. "If God is our number one priority, the next question we have to ask is, 'What steps will we take to reflect God as number one?' "

Under the statement he had written, he colored in three bullet points. "Let's think of three ways we can make God number one in our lives." It was obvious Owen was enjoying this exercise with Norah. He offered the first bullet point, "I must pray on a daily basis to the Lord."

Norah jumped in at that moment and said, "I must study the Scriptures on a daily basis." Owen wrote down Norah's exact words.

Owen added, "We must commit to worship weekly with other believers." This really was a huge one for them because they weren't always consistent in church attendance. They always found an excuse to skip out. They had lost count how many times they blamed their skipping church on one of the kids. For example, if one of them coughed just a little bit they would assume they couldn't go to church because the kids were sick. Of course, come ten in the morning the children were outside playing on the swing set.

"All right," Norah encouraged, as she sat up next to Owen on the bed. She had already turned in for the night until Owen came in wanting to devise a priority list. "Our second priority must be this marriage.

Owen wrote, *Marriage is our second priority.* He then began to color in another set of three bullet points while asking out loud, "How can we make sure marriage is a priority in our lives?"

"We could spend more time with one another," Norah suggested.

"What if we tried to go out on a date, just the two of us, once every two weeks?" Owen asked.

"That sounds good to me."

"How about this one," Norah said excitedly. "We eat supper at home together at least three out of seven nights. I know sometimes you don't have a choice about working overtime. But more times than not, you do."

Owen reluctantly agreed and wrote the bullet point down slowly. He knew the week ahead was going to be a difficult one.

"Hey," Norah said, "do you remember the sermon Pastor Schaeffer gave about prayer?"

Owen looked up and to the left trying to remember. "I don't. What was it about?"

"I can't remember the entire message, but I do remember he talked about how he and Addi would pray together regularly."

Owen could feel his heart beating out of his chest. "Well that's what preachers do. I don't know if regular people like us do that."

Norah was really enjoying the exercise at this point. "Since we have already kind of started, we could commit to praying together . . . let's say, three times a week. This would even combine our number one and number two priorities," she said enthusiastically.

About that time the door to their room opened up. Their youngest child had been getting out of the bed all night. "It's your turn," Owen said. Norah got out of bed and took her child to his room.

"Saved by the bell," Owen thought to himself. I was just hoping I could put 'have sex three nights a week' on bullet point number three. Norah walked back into the room and climbed back in bed.

"All right, so does that make three ways to keep our marriage a priority?" She asked taking the yellow notepad out of his hands to look it over. "You didn't write down 'pray together three times a week,'" she said.

"I was waiting for you to come back," he responded. "I didn't want to write anything without you in here. Remember we are one," he commented laughing. He took the note pad back and wrote down their third point. "Should we go ahead and pray together tonight?" He asked, wanting to scratch that off the list as soon as possible.

"Yeah, that sounds good." Norah said as she took Owen's hand and closed her eyes.

"Wait a minute. How do we do this?" Owen asked. He could not think of anytime in his life when he was more nervous or embarrassed. "Why don't you lead tonight and I will next time."

"Oh, no," Norah responded without opening her eyes. "Pastor Schaeffer said you were the spiritual leader. I think you should lead the prayer. I wouldn't want to infringe upon your leadership," she said with a smirk. Truth of the matter was she was too nervous to pray aloud, too.

Owen closed his eyes while clutching his wife's hand. His nervousness caused sweat to bead up on his palms, and he knew Norah was aware of it. He began to pray, "Dear Lord," he cleared his throat, "I want to ask you to be with our marriage. Amen."

Letting go of Norah's hand, he began to wipe his sweaty palms off on the covers of the bed. He had given presentations at work in front of twenty people before and never sensed such stage fright as at that moment. Norah leaned over and gave Owen a gentle kiss on the cheek.

"Good night," she said as she rolled over and covered up for the night.

"Night," Owen responded as he got under the covers to call it a night. That one short prayer took a lot out of him.

They were both just about to go to sleep when Norah's phone vibrated and then beeped. Norah's heart stopped beating. "Surely, he isn't texting me this late at night." She hoped Owen wouldn't ask about it.

"Did someone just text you?"

"Yeah," her mind raced frantically to come up with a story, "Its Samantha at the salon. She said she would text me what time I could go in tomorrow."

"Didn't you just have your hair done?"

"Yeah, but she ran out of highlights. She wanted me to come back in so she could finish the job."

"Oh," Owen said as he opened his mouth, fighting back an exhausted yawn. "Well, good night."

He bought it. She leaned over and read the text. "Thinking of you," Allen had written. She starred at the ceiling fan for two hours wondering what she was going to do about Allen.

CHAPTER FIVE

Wednesday afternoon came quickly. Owen picked Norah up from the house, and they headed to meet Pastor Schaeffer. Owen's mind was still engaged in the last meeting he attended at work. He was overwhelmingly preoccupied as he drove in virtual silence.

"What are you thinking about?" Norah asked.

"Nothing, we just had a rough meeting, that's all. I am thinking of all the things I should have said, but I didn't."

"Look, there's Pastor Schaeffer." Norah said as they pulled into the parking lot. "What is he doing?"

Pastor Schaeffer was walking toward them holding a yellow box. As they parked, Schaeffer walked around to open the door for Norah. "You are right on time. Addi told me to tell you how much she enjoyed getting to spend time with you the other night. In fact, you both remind us a little of ourselves."

Walking around toward the front of the vehicle, Owen asked, "What's with the yellow box?"

"Inside this yellow box?" He asked, holding it up as if there were a parking lot full of yellow boxes. "Let's go in and we will find out."

Pastor Schaeffer opened the door to the church office allowing Owen and Norah to walk in first. "Just make your way back to my office, and we can begin."

After they had all settled into their seats, Pastor Schaeffer put the box on the center of his desk and opened it up. "After yellow comes green," Pastor said with a smile on his face. "And yellow, while not easy, is better than red."

"So do you have another set of cards in there?" Owen asked.

"Sure do."

"Twenty bucks says the cards are yellow, right?" Owen asked.

"I am not a betting man, Owen." Pastor Schaeffer said with a serious tone, starring intently into Owen's eyes. About the time Owen felt overwhelmingly awkward, Pastor Schaeffer let out a belly laugh, "I'm just kidding. Of course they are yellow."

Norah chuckled while Owen let out a nervous laugh.

"The first card deals primarily with what we spoke about at our house." He read the morning statement on the card aloud, "I will intentionally make marriage a priority today."

Norah spoke up. "Pastor Schaeffer, you would be proud of Owen. After we left your house, we went home, and that night Owen lead us to make a priority list. Our number one priority was God and our second was our marriage. He even led us in a prayer together."

"You prayed with one another?" Pastor Schaeffer asked.

"It was a short and simple prayer. But, yes, we did pray." Owen responded as he saw Pastor Schaeffer respond with a look of pride.

"Well praise the Lord!" Pastor Schaeffer said leaning back in his chair with a look of genuine pride. Leaning forward he asked Owen, "Were you nervous about praying with Norah?"

"Not that bad."

"Not that bad?" Norah asked as she gently nudged Owen on the shoulder. "Your palms were sweating so bad you had to drink a Gatorade."

"Okay, okay. Yes, I was a little nervous." Owen admitted, looking at the floor.

"Guess what?" Pastor Schaeffer asked in a rhetorical fashion. "I get nervous every single time I start to pray with Addi."

Owen looked up tilting his head slightly to the right in disbelief. "It's true. I know the Pastor shouldn't be nervous about praying with his wife. But, Pastor or not, we all face the same attack prior to praying. We feel--how should I say it--a little self-conscious when we start to pray. That's normal. You see, the enemy doesn't want any married couple to pray. He knows it honors God and helps the marriage grow. So he will attack you and make you think all sorts of things when you pray. The real man is the one who follows through with the prayer. If it were simple, everyone would do it."

That made sense to both Norah and Owen. As a result, Owen felt some relief and even a greater appreciation for the transparency of his Pastor. He had assumed Pastors never faced difficulty in spiritual matters. "So what else does the card say?" Norah asked, breaking the silence.

"Well, in order to break inconsistent priorities, you have to be on the offense. Therefore, you begin your day in prayer asking God to help you keep your marriage a priority. The verse that helps you throughout the day is Philippians 2:3."

Pastor Schaeffer opened his Bible to the verse and handed it to Norah. "Read that out loud for us."

Norah began to read.

Do nothing from selfishness or empty conceit, but with humility of mind regard one another as more important than yourselves.--Philippians 2:3

Pastor Schaeffer launched into a mini-sermon. "Paul was writing to a church which was caught up in selfishness. Their fellowship was being attacked by this, and Paul wrote directly to their situation. When you continue to read Philippians 2, you will find that Paul uses Jesus as the supreme example of someone who put others before himself. Now, although this verse was written explicitly to a church, the principle we learn can be applied to our marriages. In order for your marriage to be unified, you have to live unselfishly by properly setting your priorities."

Picking up the card, he read the next characteristic of yellow, "*Iffy love. Iffy love* is simply conditional love," he explained. "The husband will love the wife if she meets his set of mostly unspoken standards. The wife will love the husband if he meets her set of mostly unspoken standards. The reality is that love within a Christian marriage cannot be iffy love. It cannot be conditionally based upon a feeling, goose bumps, hot flashes or whatever. Ultimately, love is based upon a choice. We must choose to love our spouse unconditionally."

Owen and Norah listened with undivided attention.

"God chose to love us based upon no condition whatsoever. He did not look to see who could meet His standards so that they might be qualified to receive his love. The Scripture states in Romans 5:8, 'God demonstrated his love in this, that while we were yet sinners Christ died for us.' Although God saw us as sinners who could not merit His love, He chose to love us."

Looking at Norah, he asked a simple question, "Norah, where would you be if God's love was iffy love?"

"That's a pretty easy question to answer. I'd still be lost and in a mess."

"You are exactly right." Schaeffer replied, "And that is exactly where your marriage will be if you choose iffy love--lost and in a mess."

"Well how will we know if iffy love is what we are using?" Owen asked.

"That is a great question, Owen. The greatest temptation is to have a critical attitude toward your spouse. Whenever you are critical toward your spouse, you are expressing conditional love."

"A couple of years ago I counseled a couple who seemed to get stuck in yellow. The problem was that the wife was always critical of the husband. I'll never forget it. She didn't like the way he dressed. So she criticized. She didn't like the way he talked. So she criticized. She didn't even like the way he sat in a chair. I remember she spent five minutes talking to me about how bad he slouched in his chair. She had placed all of these conditions on her husband. It was driving him crazy. My goodness, I was in the room with her for only thirty minutes, and she was driving me crazy!" he said with a laugh.

"Most often a critical attitude shows up in a marriage when there is comparison. For example, the husband compares his wife with the models he sees on television. The wife compares her husband with her best friend's husband. Comparing anything in life is a recipe for disaster."

Pastor Schaeffer leaned back in his chair and became very transparent again. "I remember when I first started preaching, I used to compare my preaching with the preaching of others. I would hear some guy preach a sermon that was dull and hard to understand, and then think to myself, 'Our church is so blessed to have me.' On the other hand, I would hear a preacher preach a message with great clarity, power, and conviction. His church was massive and they were reaching their community for Christ. Then I would double over in depression, realizing how poor a preacher I was. Then I would think, 'I can't believe my church allows me to take the pulpit.'

"You see, Owen and Norah, comparison most often leads to either pride or self-pity. Either way, comparison always leads to disaster. And hey, no man wants to come home to a nagging wife. Proverbs 27:15 is a verse I have never quoted at home out of fear of

Addi's response. But the verse says, 'A constant dripping on a day of steady rain and a contentious woman are alike.' "

Owen had known Norah to nag a good bit. But he wouldn't dare say a word about it to Pastor Schaeffer. "So I guess there is a verse that will help us to keep from comparing."

"Yes, there is." He asked Norah to hand his Bible to Owen. "Just turn over one page, Owen, and read Philippians 4:8:

Finally, brethren, whatever is true, whatever is honorable, whatever is right, whatever is pure, whatever is lovely, whatever is of good repute, if there is excellence and if anything worthy of praise dwell on these things.—Philippians 4:8

Pastor Schaeffer began to expound. "The key to not expressing iffy love is to focus your attention on that which is right and good about your spouse. What we think about will always show up in our attitudes and actions. So you have to choose to love unconditionally and to focus on the positive aspects.. Your prayer goal in the morning is this: 'I will dwell on that which is good today.' At the end of the day, with your journal you ask the question, "How has my thought life strengthened my marriage today?"

"Pastor Schaeffer," Norah interrupted, "forgive me for interrupting. But I think you forgot to give us the evening question for inconsistent priorities."

"You are right. I totally forgot. So in the evening you ask first, 'How have I made my marriage a priority today?' Then you move on to asking, 'How has my thought life strengthened my marriage today?' "

Pastor Schaeffer got his Bible back from Owen and laid it on his desk. He then invited Owen and Norah to follow him into the worship center. As they walked toward the entrance they were overcome by curiosity. "All right, you see this?" He pointed toward the kneeling altar at the base of the stage. "This is an altar. A mentor of mine once told me if you ever need your life to be altered, visit the altar. Your marriage will be as strong as your prayer life. I am going to leave you both in here to pray with one another. Norah, I want Owen to open in prayer; then I want you to close."

"Do we kneel at the altar?" Owen asked looking around the worship center.

"There will be no one in here for the next two hours. You have the whole place to yourself. I am going to encourage you to kneel together and pray. When you are done you may leave. Oh yeah, Addi and I want to have you over to the house in two weeks. We can assess your progress in the yellow on that evening. Owen, I'll e-mail you with the details."

"Sounds good, thanks," Owen responded as they both watched Pastor Schaeffer leave the worship center, the door closing quietly behind him.

Norah looked at Owen for leadership. He took responsibility, "Well, I guess we need to kneel here and pray. Norah, is there anything I can pray for you about?"

CHAPTER SIX

The very next night Norah sat in the bed with her journal in front of her. She was still thinking of Allen. In fact, she checked her phone twice that day just to see if he had sent any texts to her. She knew it was wrong, but an inner desire seemed to take over. Realizing she was in a daydream, she shook her head and refocused on the yellow card. "Have I made my marriage a priority today?" She wrote in her journal a prayer to God.

God,

I can't keep my mind off him. I know it is wrong but . . . I know there is no excuse. Owen is making great progress, and I am thankful for what you are doing in his life. You have helped us into the yellow. I thought Owen was the one who was the problem; however, now I know I have a huge problem as well. What should I do about the text messages? Should I just continue to ignore them? I don't think I have the strength to do so. What should I do? This is keeping me from making my marriage a priority.

The next day dragged on slowly as Norah took care of the children. She had a perfect plan. Norah was meeting a few friends at the park so their children could play together. She would let her children play until they were completely exhausted. Following that, they would go home, and she could put them in the bed for a long afternoon nap. Norah grabbed her cell phone before going out to the park. She could not shake the statement which seemed to be tattooed on her mind since the middle of the night, "Get a new number."

She remembered her prayer the night before. She had asked the Lord to tell her what to do with Allen. "Surely, God is not telling me to get a new phone number. Is that really His answer?"

"What will you do, Norah?" her friend asked her. Norah was caught off guard. She hadn't been listening to the conversation of her friends. She was too busy questioning the tattoo in her mind. "Earth to Norah!" Her friend said sarcastically.

"What? I'm sorry. I have a ton on my mind. What were we talking about?" Norah acted interested.

"Oh nothing, we were just talking about the new television show which started last night."

Norah noticed one of her children falling from the swing. "That's not good." She said as she jumped from her seat to see about her oldest. "Are you okay?" Through the tears she concluded now was the time for them to head on home so she could put them in their beds.

As she left her friends and headed toward the vehicle, she continued to wonder about her phone. She was driving home when she seemingly, without even trying, drove right into the parking lot of her cell service provider. She got her children out of the van and went in. She summoned the clerk and explained, "How are you? I need to have a new number issued to me."

"Ma'am, is there something wrong with your old number?" he asked her.

"No… well… yes. There is something terribly wrong with the old number. It keeps getting me in trouble." Norah said.

"In trouble? The clerk asked with some confusion. "What do you mean 'in trouble?' "

"I don't mean to be rude, but could you just give me a new number. I have two children here who will be crying their little eyes out in a minute. I need you to give me a new number."

"No problem." After completing the necessary paper work, he inserted a new SIM chip.

While leaving the cellular store, she called Owen. Her phone call went straight to voice-mail. "Owen, this is Norah. I have a new number. You will need to save this number I just called you with into your phone. I'll explain why I did this when you come home. I love you."

Meanwhile, at the office Owen had just run into a huge problem of his own. He met a new colleague who is stationed in south Florida for the first time. The man was dressed nicely in a pen stripped suit with no tie. In his hand he had a briefcase which he placed on the conference table. He extended his hand to Owen.

"It is great to finally meet you, Owen. Ever since I took this new position, everyone has been telling me I needed to meet you."

"Well, it is good to meet you as well. You know all there is about the project by now I'm sure. You have been briefed, right?" Owen asked.

"I sure have."

"Well, let's get to it; we have a ton to do in a very short time if we are to close this deal," Owen said as he sat at the head of the conference table. All of a sudden the new pin stripped man's phone rang. It wasn't any ring though; it was some eighties love song playing as the ring tone.

The new employee blushed a little as he rushed to get his phone. He stood to his feet and said, "I am so sorry," reaching for his phone he said, "I have to take this."

Owen, motioned for him to go ahead as he walked out of the room for a few minutes. "Some star worker--the first meeting we have together and he gets up to answer his telephone. And what was with that ring?"

"Forgive me, that was my wife calling on the phone. Hence the ring tone. She and I have been married for seventeen years, and the song you just heard was our song. We danced to it on our first date, and we have always just held on to that moment as the one when we first knew . . . well you don't want to hear some sappy love story. Anyway, one of the ways we help keep our marriage a priority is to be certain we always answer the phone when the other is calling, no matter what. So where were we?"

"Do you have any children?" Owen asked.

"Sure do," opening his briefcase he pulled out a small picture album. "We have three boys and a girl." Owen was wondering what kind of man carried a picture album in his briefcase. "I am probably the luckiest man on earth. My wife is more beautiful now than when we first met, and our children are a huge blessing to us."

Thumbing through the pictures, Owen continued to have a conversation with himself. "Good grief, she is pretty," he thought. "Look at them. They seem to have it all together. I wonder why I don't think Norah is prettier now than ever before."

"That's a picture of us all rappelling in the mountains. My wife is kind of an adventurous woman. We had a blast that day."

"Well it looks like you were having a great day," Owen said, still thinking Norah would never do anything adventurous. She is so plain. "Hold on just a minute," Owen said, "I just remembered I forgot a file in my office."

Exiting the conference room, he realized he was doing exactly what he was not supposed to be doing. He was comparing his marriage to that of some stranger he just met. As he was mentally driving down "pity lane" headed for "disaster falls," he found the yellow card on his desk. He kept it under a big stack of books so no one would see it. He looked at his verse: Philippians 4:8. Closing the door of his office he prayed audibly, "God, forgive me for downplaying the marriage you have given me. Forgive me for comparing Norah to some random lady. Help me to keep my mind focused." He grabbed a file from his desk and went back into the conference room.

"All right then," placing the file beneath a stack of papers, Owen said, "let's get started."

After their meeting, which went very well, Owen got in his truck and headed home. He realized he missed a phone call from an unknown number on his cell. When he checked his voice message, he heard Norah's voice. "Why did she get a new number?"

His children tackled him as soon as he walked through the front door. Holding one while wrestling with the other he asked Norah, "What's the deal with your new phone number?"

"Kids, your supper is ready. Come in and eat." After settling them down to their mac-and-cheese with chicken fingers, Norah sat down in the living room to explain to Owen what was going on. "Do you remember Allen?"

"Of course I remember Allen."

"He has been sending me text messages." Owen stood up. You could see the anger rising up to his head. "Last night I read the question, "How have I made my marriage a priority today? I asked God to help me with the phone situation. When I woke up this morning, all I could think about was getting a new phone number. So I did. I took that step to make our marriage a priority."

The last sentence out of her mouth didn't seem to settle his rage. "I can't believe you gave him your number to begin with. How would you like it if I went around giving my number to a bunch of women? I can't believe you." Owen said with obvious disgust in his voice.

Norah began to cry as Owen entered their bedroom, slamming the door. She tried to get herself together so she could go help the children. Owen sat down on a chair, heartbroken, with that ridiculous eighties love song playing in his head. He grabbed his notebook and began to write his answer to the first question in the form of a prayer.

Father,

I am about to go crazy. I made my marriage a priority today by being certain I was home in time for supper. But I am crazy right now about this issue with Allen.

He read the next question on the yellow card and continued to write.

My thought life was clean today. I do remember making that crazy comparison. However, you helped me to stop by using your Word.

His anger began to subside as he wrote the following:

Norah took action today to make our marriage a priority, but I blew up at her. I have made some huge mistakes in this marriage, too, but she has been forgiving. Help me to hold my wife up during this step she is taking to better our marriage.

He put the pen down and walked back into the kitchen. Norah looked down at her food, afraid that wrath would follow his footsteps. She felt his hands touch her shoulders. Then the unexpected happened. He kissed her on the top of the head and said, "I love you."

Stunned to say the least, she responded, "I love you, too."

"I saved your new number in my phone."

CHAPTER SEVEN

"Norah, come look at this!" Owen shouted from the computer room.

"What is it?"

"It's an e-mail from Pastor Schaeffer. We are to meet him at his house this Thursday evening. He already called our baby-sitter and set up the appointment for us, paid in full."

"Are you kidding me?" Norah read the e-mail out loud. "Well, that was nice."

"It sure was, only one problem. I have a huge meeting with Jenson, our new 'star-employee' from south Florida."

"Oh," Norah said with a deflated voice.

Just then Owen remembered the ring-tone and the comment Jenson made about keeping his marriage a priority. "Don't worry though; I'll reschedule the meeting for Wednesday. That does mean I'll have to be late coming in tomorrow evening because there are some things that I have to do to be prepared."

"I'll keep your food warm for you." Norah responded with a sense of joy. Owen stood up and they both embraced.

Thursday evening came and the babysitter was there right on time as usual. "Pastor Schaeffer already paid me. You must be doing some great service at the church for that to happen. I bet there will be a special place in heaven for you," she said jokingly as she picked up the youngest child.

Owen quickly remarked, "If there is a special place in heaven for anyone, it will be for you. I mean you have to take care of these wild children while we are gone."

"Everything you need is on the counter. The kids may try to talk you into letting them stay up late. Don't be fooled; they are dead tired. They napped for only about fifteen minutes today." Norah said.

"Okay, I'll see you later," said the babysitter.

Addison opened the door of her home to greet her two new friends. As she did before, she hugged Norah and said, "It is so good to see you." Looking at Owen, she hugged him as well.

"I don't know if you can top the last meal you made, Mrs. Addison. That was some good cooking," Owen said.

"I made my mother's secret spaghetti sauce for tonight. So if it's not good, we will blame it on my mother," she said laughing.

"It doesn't have tomatoes in it, does it?" Owen said. "Because Norah is deathly allergic to tomatoes."

"Oh, no, Norah! I had no idea."

"You believe that?" Norah laughed.

"You had me going on that one, Owen. Schaeffer, they are here, Honey, and Owen brought some jokes with him, too." Pastor Schaeffer was upstairs putting the final sentence on Sunday's message.

"Great," Pastor said as he walked down the stairs. "How have you been doing?"

Norah responded first, "We have actually been doing quite well. We had our ups and downs, but, the yellow cards are working." Norah walked into the kitchen to help Addison with the food.

"I'll be honest, Pastor," Owen said quietly in the living room. "I really thought the journal, reading the Bible, and praying would be a bit effeminate, but it has turned out to be the exact opposite. God has really helped me tremendously."

"If I had a dollar for every time a man said something along those lines, we could build a new worship center." Pastor Schaeffer continued, "The Scriptures teach us to work out our spiritual life. In fact, Paul uses the imagery of working out with weights. In the same way a man works out to gain muscle, a man has to work out to be spiritually strong. That is exactly what is happening to you. You are gaining spiritual strength."

About that time Norah said, "Okay, men, the food is ready."

They all took the same seats they had last time they were over. Owen put his napkin in his lap when Pastor Schaeffer called on him to say the blessing.

"You want *me* to say the blessing?" Owen asked.

"Go ahead Honey; you can do it." Norah said.

"Well, I know I can do it. I'm just not used to doing it with a man of the cloth in front of me," he joked to ease the tension. "Let's pray."

Owen started in on the prayer. "Dear Lord, we are so grateful for this meal you have placed before us by your divine grace. We want to give honor to Thee as we eat tonight. We beseech Thee to bless this food to the nourishment of our bodies. Amen."

"What in the world was that?" Norah asked looking at Owen with a stunned look on her face.

"What was what?"

"Amen," Pastor Schaeffer said. "That was great King's English."

Addison, trying not to laugh, took a sip of her tea. Schaeffer caught her eye though, and she burst out with laughter. She spit tea all over the table. Norah fell out laughing, too. Owen finally said, "I was trying to sound dignified in front of the Pastor here. Give me a break!"

They all laughed and then began to eat. "This spaghetti is great!" Owen said.

Norah followed, "If it would not trouble you, I may beseech thee for another plate full in a moment." They laughed again.

That night was different with Pastor Schaeffer and his wife. They spent some time getting to know one another over supper. Owen even started to enjoy hanging out with Schaeffer. Norah and Owen both found out that the Pastor and his wife were the kind of people they would enjoy spending more time with.

They talked about their journey in the yellow for just a moment. Norah explained her phone story and Owen's shocking response. Owen shared for the first time his story about being in the office with Jenson and his ring tone. The night went well. "So what's the next color?" Owen asked.

"I see the progress you are both making, and it makes me extremely happy. However, I want to hold off for a few days on the green. Moving from yellow to green is a huge step. I don't want you to get overwhelmed. So let's meet again in my office next Wednesday afternoon and assess whether or not you are ready for green."

"That sounds good to me," Norah responded. "I am kind of enjoying the yellow marriage."

"It sure beats red, doesn't it?" Addison responded.

Pastor Schaeffer slipped a sealed yellow envelope to Owen and said, "Take your wife out and open this on your date. Do not open it before then." Owen stuck the envelope in his back pocket, promising he wouldn't open it until they went out on their date.

Owen and Norah left the Schaeffer's house that night greatly encouraged by their time together. They drove home that night and settled down for bed. After their prayer together, Owen said, "Tomorrow night let's go out on a date."

"That's a great idea."

The next morning Owen quickly got ready for work. He looked over his yellow cards before leaving. He read the statement: "I will intentionally make my marriage a priority today." He took out his day-planner and made two tasks for himself. Task number one: e-mail a love note to Norah today. Task number two: pick up flowers for the date.

He hugged his family before leaving for work, and told Norah he loved her. "I can't wait for tonight" he said.

"Me either. I'll get mom to come and watch the kids for us."

He got to the office that morning and began working on his tasks. He had an appointment at 10 A.M. and seven tasks which had to be done prior to the meeting. He scanned down his list and chose to write Norah first.

```
Norah,

This past month has been great. I know
not everything we have faced has been
wonderful. However, I feel like I am
closer to you at this moment than ever
before. I want you to know I love you with
all of my heart. You are everything to
me. I am looking forward to tonight.

Love,

Owen
```

After pressing "send" on his computer, he knocked out his other tasks in no time. In fact, he had an extra fifteen minutes left over. He grabbed a cup of coffee and reviewed his notes before the meeting.

CHAPTER EIGHT

"Why am I so nervous?" Norah said to herself as she was getting ready for the big date. She had taken the children with her that morning to pick out a brand new dress for the event. Her mother, who lives one town over from her, agreed to take the children after their naps and let them spend the night with her. Norah had a total of two hours to get ready. The biggest dilemma she faced in getting dressed was what pair of shoes she should wear.

Standing in front of the mirror with her black high heels on, she wondered if it were a sad attempt at trying to look younger or even worse, sexy. She kicked off the high heels and tried on the black flats. The only problem with these is that they made her look old, short, and unsexy. "I'll figure this out later," she said out loud as she began to apply her make up.

Her stomach was in knots over their soon coming adventure, and she was filled with confusion. "This is my husband. I shouldn't be nervous to go on a date with my husband. We sleep in the same bed every night, for crying out loud." As she twisted her lipstick up she realized she was almost out. There was just enough for two, maybe three, more applications.

She had just finished getting ready when the doorbell rang. "Who would be ringing our doorbell?" She ran to the door and looked through the peep hole. "What are you doing here?" she shouted. Owen was holding a long stemmed rose in his hand. "Hold on just a minute!" Norah ran back into her room grabbed the black flats and through them to the back of the closet. She slipped on the high heels, brushed her dress down flat and took one more look in the mirror.

The door opened slowly, and Owen took a long look at Norah. In fact, he looked her down and up twice before speaking a word.

"Well, you didn't think I was going to wear some _old_ dress for this night did you?"

He reached out and gave her the rose saying, "This is for you. Norah, you look absolutely beautiful. He stepped in close and wrapped his arms around her." At that moment a new attraction to his wife seemed to spark. In fact, it may have sparked a little too much. "You just want to stay in tonight?"

"Are you kidding me? I got dressed up to go out on a date. Besides, we have all night. The kids are spending the night with my mom."

His eyes got big, and a huge smile came across his face. "We have reservations tonight at the Palm Bay Restaurant. I know they serve your favorite pecan chicken."

He took her hand and they walked to the vehicle. He opened her door as he did when they first started dating.

As they entered the restaurant, Owen reached into his back left pocket. He was making sure the yellow letter discreetly given to him by Pastor Schaeffer was still there. As soon as they sat down, he pulled out the letter and said, "Look what I have!"

"Who is that from?"

"Pastor Schaeffer gave it to me last night as we were leaving his house. He told me I was not allowed to open it until we go on our date."

Norah's curiosity, mixed with a little anxiety, made her say with excitement, "Let's open it."

He tore the letter open from the top quite meticulously so as to not rip the note that was inside. He read the letter, typed by Pastor Schaeffer so Norah could hear.

I am extremely proud of what God is doing in your marriage. I chose not to give you the third characteristic of the yellow until you were both together on this date. (You'd better be on a date.)

The third characteristic of yellow is "inconsiderate choices." These choices can show up practically anywhere. Your finances, your speech, your intimate lives, etc. are all areas where inconsiderate choices can be made.

I want you to discuss two areas where inconsiderate choices have been made in your marriage. This is not to start a feud, but rather to invite open discussion about how to better your marriage.

Inconsiderate choices always cause division between married couples. The temptation would be to make choices which cause disunity.

I'll give you an example of my inconsiderate choice with Addi. I never knew this bothered her until someone asked us to have this discussion. When she and I traveled anywhere and we stopped at a convenience store for gas, I would go inside and pay the cashier. More often than not, I would get myself a Coke. That seems innocent enough, right?

The problem is that I wouldn't get Addi anything. I would just go back to the car sipping on my Coke. Now don't get me wrong. I would offer her a sip, but I knew she wasn't a fan of Coke.

She always declined, and then didn't speak for the rest of the trip. I would ask, "Honey, are you all right?" She would just say, "Yes," but she continued to look out the window.

When we were asked to discuss our inconsiderate choices, she immediately brought this up. I never knew it bothered her. However, my choice was causing division. So now, when I enter a convenience store to get a Coke, I always ask her if she would like something to drink.

Small choices we make hold the potential to stall our marriage in the yellow. This all stems back to selfishness and a new verse to fight it, "Give preference to one another in honor."--Romans 12:10b. The journal question for the day is:

"How have my choices enhanced the unity
of our marriage today?"

When I see you again, we will discuss this
verse further. But for now, memorize it
and apply its principle to your marriage
and discuss your own inconsiderate
choices. (Owen, you go ahead and go
first.)

Happy Discussion,

Pastor Schaeffer

"Well, this should be a lot of fun," Owen said sarcastically.

"Well, let's not forget that everything Pastor Schaeffer has asked us to do so far has been a little awkward at first. Somehow, though, it always seems to help," Norah commented in a reassuring tone.

The waitress came up and asked them if they were ready to order. "Give us just a minute. We haven't even looked at the menu yet," Owen said.

"We can go ahead and get our drinks, though; I'll have a glass of water with lemon please," Norah stated politely.

"How about you sir?"

"I'll take a water and cup of coffee."

Owen turned his attention back to his wife. He didn't want to be the one to go first. The last thing he wanted to do was hurt her feelings at the start of the date. "You go ahead. Tell me an inconsiderate choice I make that causes disunity."

"Not so fast," Norah tilted her head, "You are supposed to go first . . . .remember."

"I know, I was hoping you forgot about that part." Owen put his elbows on the table with one hand on his chin. "Let me think. An inconsiderate choice…"

"What's wrong? You don't know where to start?" Norah asked jokingly trying to reduce the rising tension.

"Real funny. Okay, I have one. Now promise me you will not get mad at me when I share this with you." At about that time, the drinks arrived. Owen took a sip of his coffee to stall what he was about to say for another moment.

"I'll give you a specific incident. Do you remember when we were at John and Katy's house?"

"You mean two months ago?" Norah asked.

"Yeah."

"Yeah, I remember that night."

"Well, when we were all eating together, you made a couple of derogatory comments about me in front of them."

"What did I say?" Norah asked looking puzzled. She had no idea what Owen was talking about.

"I don't remember what we were talking about exactly, but you mentioned to them that I never clean up after myself. I also remember your telling them in a 'nutshell' that I was irresponsible."

"Owen, we were all kidding around. I was just joking. I know you mostly clean up after yourself and are responsible. If you were irresponsible, you wouldn't be doing so well in your job. Besides, I was just joking around."

"I know, but sometimes your jokes are mixed with a little bit of truth. That night I felt like you were taking a couple of jabs at me. In fact, it pretty much made me feel…" He paused for a moment.

"Feel what?"

"Never mind."

"No, tell me. I want to know."

"It embarrassed me," Owen said, realizing he was embarrassed even admitting this to Norah. "I just don't like to be painted with a negative brush in front of people."

"Well," Norah said with honesty, "I am really sorry. If I had known it was going to hurt your feelings, I would have never said it. I will be absolutely certain to not make that mistake again. I really had no idea. Now I know why you gave me the silent treatment the rest of the night."

"Oh yeah, I forgot about the silent treatment." The silent treatment was Owen's way of showing his disapproval of pretty much any situation. "Now it's your turn. Tell me about an inconsiderate choice I have made."

"I have two."

"Good grief, Norah, this is worse than a performance review at work."

"The first inconsiderate choice has to do with your clothes."

"My clothes! You don't like what I wear?"

"No, it doesn't have to do with what you wear, but where you put what you wear after you are done wearing them. I clean the house up every week from top to bottom. Practically every time, I have to pick up a pile of your clothes you have stacked on the floor beside the bed. It's like you couldn't care less about what I'm doing. I start to feel unappreciated; I start to feel like your personal maid."

"You know I appreciate you, Norah."

"How would I know that? You never say anything."

"Good point" Owen agreed. He couldn't remember the last time he thanked Norah for the job she does around the house. "I'll stop stacking my clothes up on the floor. Do you forgive me?"

"Of course."

"Hit me with number two."

"You sure?"

"Of course I'm sure."

Norah squeezed a lemon slice into her ice water. "I know you work hard, and when you come in, you are extremely tired. However, I am tired too. After supper you usually go sit in your chair and relax. I'm stuck cleaning up the kitchen, giving baths to the children, and then putting them in the bed. I would love it if you could help me with these chores every once in a while."

"I never even thought about helping you." Owen could see clearly his inconsiderate choice and wanted to make an action plan to fix it. "Tell you what. From now on we will take turns cleaning up the kitchen and bathing the kids. How does that sound?"

"That sounds great. You don't have to do it every time, just every once in a while would be helpful."

"If its every once in a while, it will never become a habit. Let's just say from now on. But I get to choose which I want to do."

"That sounds fair to me." Norah felt relived that Owen didn't give a rebuttal to either one of her statements. They ordered their food soon after that and enjoyed their time together for the rest of the evening.

CHAPTER NINE

They took their same places in Pastor Schaeffer's office, ready to discuss their marriage in the yellow. "Did you enjoy your date?"

"We sure did," Owen responded, "We even enjoyed the yellow note you gave us."

"Praise the Lord. The verse I gave you comes from Paul's writings. Again, this verse is directed to Christians as it pertains to the usage of their spiritual service toward one another. They were to give preference to one another in honor."

"So the principle applied to marriage is that I am supposed to give precedence to Owen. Right?"

"Norah, you got it. Sounds like things are going well with you both. I can't tell you the difference between your attitudes now compared to your attitudes when you first set foot in this office. I love seeing marriages advance from one color to the next."

"I love seeing Owen clean up the kitchen!"

"What are you talking about?"

"One of the inconsiderate choices I make..." Owen restated, "One of the inconsiderate choices I *made* was leaving Norah to clean the kitchen, bathe the kids, and put them to bed. I never realized that was causing disunity. We discussed it over our date and made a plan to take turns cleaning and bathing."

"That sounds just like Addi and me. When she and I were first married, she worked a full time job as well as I with the church. When we got home, Addi would cook and clean. I would sit." Norah punched Owen on the arm. "That's right, Owen, you aren't the only dumb man," Pastor Schaeffer laughed.

"Addi finally told me my choice was causing problems. So we wrote down the names of all our rooms in the house on little sheets of paper. On Saturday we put the names of the rooms into a hat and drew. Whichever rooms we drew, we cleaned. You should have seen Addi praying she didn't get the bathrooms. She hated cleaning the bathrooms. In fact, when she drew the bathrooms, I could trade her three other rooms for them. It was hilarious."

"It really is amazing how small choices we make in our marriages hold the potential to cause so much friction," Owen said.

"You got that right, brother," Pastor Schaeffer said.

"So are we ready for the green?" Norah asked. She had actually begun to enjoy the adventure.

"I believe you are," Pastor replied. A knock came at the Pastor's office door. "Yes, Ma'am?" Schaeffer asked.

"I am so sorry to bother you, but Addison is on the line. She wanted to speak to you."

"Okay." Pastor Schaeffer turned his attention to Owen and Norah. "Do you mind if I take this real quick?"

"You should always take your wife's phone calls. It shows she is a priority," Owen remarked.

"He learned that all by himself!" Norah said laughing and offering a high five to Owen.

"Hello." Pastor Schaeffer started. He sat there and nodded his head up and down signaling _yes_. "That's a great idea, Addi. You are the brains, and I am the brawn. I'm sitting right here with Owen and Norah so I'll talk with them about it. I'll be home in about thirty minutes. I love you." Pastor Schaeffer hung up the phone.

"Two weeks from this Thursday Addi wants to have you over again for supper. How does that sound?" Pastor Schaeffer asked Owen and Norah.

Owen reached in his pocket and pulled out his Blackberry. "I am putting it down right now. Looks good to me."

"We will have to have you over to the house sometime. I feel like a free-loader. We are always eating and never pitching in. Tell you what--I'll bring four of my favorite desserts," said Norah.

"You better make it six. Addi has invited another couple. . . Let's talk about what a marriage looks like in the green." Owen and Norah left wondering why another couple was invited to their next meeting.

PART III:

MARRIAGE IN THE GREEN

"Wait a minute," Owen spoke up, "is there no green box?"

"Of course there is a green box. You're sitting on it," Schaeffer said with a grin. Owen stood up and looked at his chair. He looked back at the Pastor, confused. "Look under your chair."

Prior to their meeting Pastor Schaeffer had taken the green box and actually taped it under the seat. He figured this would be a good way to make the green box kind of fun. Owen reached under and took the box.

"I know, I know. Addi tells me I am corny with the boxes. But you know, while it may be corny to everybody else, it is kind of humorous to me. Let's put it this way. . .you will never forget the green box, will you? Hand it over here."

Norah gave a courtesy laugh and sarcastically said, "That was real funny."

"You're starting to sound like Addi now," Schaeffer said laughing. "Green and blue are slightly different from red and yellow. Red and yellow have three major descriptions. Green and blue have only two major descriptions."

"Does that mean we have only two verses to memorize?" Owen asked wittily.

"You are correct, sir. But these new verses come at a great price."

"Are you charging us now?" Norah asked looking at Owen for an expected laugh.

"Of course not. But the green will cost you your life." Pastor Schaeffer said seriously as he opened the box and pulled out the card.

"What do you mean . . . our lives?" Owen said scratching the back of his head nervously.

"Well as you progress through the colors, you find that you continue to lose the *old you* as you gradually put on the *new you.*" He looked down at the card and read aloud. "Marriage in the green describes a couple who is Spirit-controlled." He reached for his Bible and handed it to Norah. "Norah, I want you to read Ephesians 5:18-21. Owen, I want you to scoot over closer to her so you can see the verses as well."

She quickly found the passage and began to read the verses:

And do not get drunk with wine, which is dissipation, but be filled with the Spirit, speaking to one another in psalms and hymns and spiritual songs, singing and making melody with your heart to the Lord; always giving thanks for all things in the name of our Lord Jesus Christ to God, even the Father; and be subject to one another in the fear of Christ.—Ephesians 5:18-21

"Good news, Pastor. We don't drink." Owen remarked after the verses were read.

"I wish it were that simple. Over half of our congregation would be filled with the Spirit then," Pastor Schaeffer said, throwing his head back in laughter. "I remember studying this passage of Scripture in our Greek New Testament class in seminary. I discovered that Paul used the verb tense, 'be filled', to speak of a continuous action. He was literally saying, 'keep on being filled with the Spirit.' Or we could even say that the follower of Christ should make being filled with the Spirit a habitual lifestyle."

Pastor Schaeffer continued, "I find it interesting that he uses this concept after saying 'don't get drunk with wine'. I have prayed with many people who have made it their habitual lifestyle to get drunk with alcohol. If you think about it, when a person is drunk, everything about them changes. In fact, let me ask you a simple question. What changes in a person when they are intoxicated?"

"Well, I know at the Christmas parties I find most of the men began to talk louder," Owen said.

"My great uncle was an alcoholic." Norah spoke up. "When he was drinking, he couldn't walk straight, think straight, or do anything else straight. He spent most of his time sitting in a broken, run down chair giving everyone his opinion."

"You're right. A person who is a drunk thinks differently, sees differently, talks differently, walks differently, and just acts completely differently. Here is where I want you to listen to very closely. Alcohol hides the real you. The Holy Spirit hides the old you."

"That's good." Owen said.

"You see, a person who is intoxicated by the Holy Spirit thinks differently, sees differently, talks differently, walks differently, and just acts completely differently. I am confident Paul was emphasizing that point in this text of Scripture." Taking a green highlighter out of his desk drawer, he handed it to Owen. "Look at the verses again and highlight the words that end in 'ing'."

"Of course the highlighter had to be green!" Norah said smiling.

"I have to keep the theme going," Pastor chuckled.

"Okay, I think I have them." Owen said as he highlighted the last word.

"What are they?"

"Speaking. Singing. Making. Giving." Owen replied.

"Very good. These are evidences in your life that you are being controlled by the Holy Spirit. Or perhaps I could say these are evidences you are a Holy Spirit-aholic. I'm sorry, that's my corniness coming back."

Pastor Schaeffer continued in his mini-sermon fashion. "When you are controlled by the Holy Spirit, you will honor God and build one another up with your words. This is what happens in a local fellowship when we speak to one another in psalms, hymns, and spiritual songs. Paul is speaking contextually about the local church. I believe the principle we find here can be applied to a marriage relationship as well."

"So our words give evidence as to whether or not we are being controlled by the Holy Spirit?" Norah asked vocalizing her thoughts.

"Exactly, Paul says something else about how we use our tongues." He motioned for the Bible and read Ephesians 4:29:

Let no unwholesome word proceed from your mouth, but only such a word as is good for edification according to the need of the moment, so that it will give grace to those who hear.—Ephesians 4:29

The terminology Paul used here for 'unwholesome word' speaks of something that is rotten, putrefied, and worthless. We are literally commanded by God not to allow any rotten, putrefied, and worthless words to exit our mouths."

"Now, I have never shared this story with anyone," Pastor Schaeffer leaned up and put his elbows on his desk. "My cell phone rang one afternoon as I was traveling home. It was a couple in the church where I served at the time. I knew them well and had become pretty close to the husband. I answered the phone and said, 'Hello.' But there was no response. I realized they had accidentally called me without realizing it. The problem is that their phone call came in the middle of a knock down, drag out argument they were having."

"Did you hang up the phone?" Norah asked moving to edge of her seat.

"Of course I did. Just not right off the bat. I listened in for a moment."

"What were they saying?" Owen asked with great interest.

"Well, to be honest, I can't repeat what they were saying because the language they used was horrible. It reminded me of this passage of Scripture. Every sentence that came out of their mouths was completely rotten, putrefied, and worthless. They continued to tear one another down over and over again. It was so bad that I actually became embarrassed for them. I had to hang up and pray first that God would help them to see the destruction they were bringing to their marriage. Then I prayed they wouldn't realize they had accidentally called me on the phone."

"Did they ever find out it was you?" Norah asked.

"I don't know. But it did change what I was preaching about on that Sunday," Pastor Schaeffer laughed. "But you get the point. Your words can tear one another down, or as you are controlled by the Holy Spirit, your words can give grace."

"What does that mean 'to give grace'?" Owen asked.

"Well look at how God gives grace to you and me. God gives grace in the sense that He saves us from our sin. But also, we find God's grace enables us to accomplish His purposes. So grace literally encourages and enables us. God desires for us to speak words of grace to our spouse. We speak words of encouragement to one another. This builds us up."

"For example," Pastor Schaeffer turned his full attention on Owen. "When you are controlled by the Spirit, your words will make Norah strong, secure, and stable." Turning his attention to Norah, Pastor Schaeffer continued, "When you are controlled by the Spirit, your words will bring confidence, encouragement, and support to Owen."

"So before either of you speaks, you should take a spiritual examination of your words. Or it could be said that you should _sniff test_ your words. Do they stink? Or do they build up? There will be times, Norah, when you would like to give Owen a piece of your mind. There will be times, Owen, when you would like to make a cutting remark to Norah. However, these are the times when you must put to death the old you and be intoxicated by the Holy Spirit."

"I have never heard anyone explain it like that before," Owen said out loud as his mind replayed some of the awful things he had said in the past to Norah.

"Me either," Norah quickly agreed.

"When you are a Spirit-controlled couple, you will build one another up. As well, our key text teaches us that we will live to lift up Christ. You see, the ultimate goal of your marriage is not that you become a happy couple. The ultimate goal of your marriage is that you become a couple that glorifies and honors God. Paul says that you will be singing and making melody in your hearts to the Lord. The only way you will continue to see the old you fade away is to have Jesus Christ become your ultimate treasure. The only way you will live with thanksgiving to Christ is to see yourself dissipating. The Spirit of God then births a heart of thanksgiving."

"When I fell in love with Addison, there was nothing anyone could do to keep me from seeing her. I spent all my money on her. I spent all my thoughts on her. I spent all my time with her. I gave her my heart."

"That is so sweet." Norah said as only a woman could.

"It sounds sweet, but the problem is that this should not have been the foundation of our marriage. My love for Christ and my melody for Him should have been, and must be, greater than my love for her and my melody for her. When Jesus is my treasure, when He is the center of my finances, the center of my thoughts, the center of my time, then, and only then, can I be the man Addison truly needs."

A great silence came over the room as Owen and Norah sat stunned in their chairs.

"You see, the green costs you everything."

CHAPTER TWO

"But it's worth it," said Norah.

"No doubt," Pastor confirmed, "When you are Spirit-controlled, you will enjoy one another's fruit. The fruit of the Spirit is love, joy, peace, patience, kindness, goodness, faithfulness, gentleness, and self control. Galatians 5:22-23."

Just then Pastor Schaeffer took out a yellow note pad and asked for the highlighter. He drew a green line down the middle of the paper and wrote the word "flesh" in one column and the word "Spirit" in the other. He took out a black ball point pen and quickly wrote the fruits of the Spirit down, and then quickly began the opposite of the fruit under the word "flesh".

Holding up the pad for Norah and Owen to see he began to explain, "When you are controlled by the old you, you will display hate, misery, turmoil, impatience, meanness, manipulation, unfaithfulness, and you will be out of control. These are the characteristics of many marriages."

"That describes a marriage in the red," Owen said beginning to better understand his role as a husband.

"Definitely, so in order to see whether or not you are Spirit-controlled or flesh-controlled all you have to do is examine your fruit." Pointing at the "flesh" column, Pastor Schaeffer commented, "No one wants to eat bad fruit. However, this is what you feed one another when you are controlled by the flesh." Pointing at the "Spirit" column, Pastor Schaeffer said, "This is what you want to serve one another."

"That makes good sense to me," Owen said sitting back in his chair allowing the truth to settle in.

"May we have that sheet of paper?" Norah asked.

Pastor Schaeffer ripped the sheet from the yellow note pad and handed it over. Norah folded the sheet in half and put it in her purse.

"You should be able to guess what the greatest temptation is concerning living a Spirit-controlled life, right?"

"I would say it is simply to be controlled by our flesh instead of by the Holy Spirit," Norah answered.

"That is exactly right. The temptation is not to be controlled by the Spirit, but to be controlled by our flesh." At that moment a gentle knock came on the door of the Pastor's office. "Come in."

"Pastor, your next appointment has just arrived." Pastor Schaeffer looked confused. He had thought Owen and Norah were the last appointment.

However, instead of asking he simply responded. "Okay. Give me ten more minutes." As his secretary shut the door, Pastor Schaeffer said, "I can't remember who I am supposed to meet with next."

"Happens to me all the time!" Owen remarked with a chuckle.

"Let's talk about the second characteristic of a marriage in the green. You will not only be Spirit-controlled, but you will also be service-oriented. In John 13 Jesus washed the feet of his disciples. Following that act of service He states, 'You ought also to wash one another's feet. For I gave you an example that you also should do as I did to you.' In the latter part of the same chapter Jesus gives a command. 'Love one another, even as I have loved you, that you also love one another.' "

"I like where this is going," Norah interrupted. "Owen gets to massage my feet."

"That's gross." Owen said jokingly. They all laughed together.

"Okay, okay. No more jokes. I have a mystery guest waiting outside." Collecting his thoughts, Pastor Schaeffer continued, "I want you to note the interesting and divine work of the Spirit of God in writing the thirteenth chapter of John. He wrote about an act of service as simple as washing, not massaging, the disciples feet; he then challenged them to love one another. So here is the conclusion: true love will be seen in your service toward one another. In fact, let's drop that into the context of marriage. True love in marriage will be evidenced by true service to your spouse."

"Now I believe there are two major ways we need to serve our spouses. We serve them automatically, and we serve them intentionally."

"Please explain." Owen commented.

"Well, Addi does most, if not all, of the grocery shopping for us. She typically purchases groceries about once every two weeks on Saturday. Well, when she pulls into the garage, she has tons of grocery bags in the back of the car. I like to lie on the couch and watch sports on Saturday. Now as she is loading the bags into the house, my automatic response is to get up from the couch and help her get all the groceries in."

"That sounds like a great idea," Norah responded playfully nudging Owen's leg. She typically unloaded all the groceries while simultaneously trying to keep the children happy.

"Intentional service is service with forethought. When I know Addi is just dog-tired, I sometimes intentionally help her out. For example, I may fill up the bath tub for her with all the perks--you know, the bubbles, candles, music, etc. I simply tell her to go upstairs and take a bath. While she is taking a bath, I will be downstairs in the kitchen making supper. When she is finished with her bath, she comes down to a table with food already prepared and ready to eat. That is intentional service."

"I don't like to take baths," Owen said jokingly.

"You are nuts, man! But I'll have to hand it to you. That was pretty funny." Pastor Schaeffer said as Norah rolled her eyes at Owen.

"Now the greatest temptation to a service-oriented marriage is just plain laziness. Being lazy will destroy your marriage. Could you imagine if I remained on the couch as Addi lugged two weeks' worth of groceries into the house? You know how I figured out I was lazy?"

"How?" Norah asked.

"Well, Addi told me I was one Saturday as I was on the couch watching football. She raised me up right."

"I need to do a better job of raising Owen." Owen responded by rolling his eyes, mocking what she had done previously.

"I may say, 'I love you', to Addi but those words seem empty if I am not showing my love."

Being time conscious, Owen looked at his watch and said, "All right, Pastor, this is the two minute warning."

"Well, take a look at the daily questions card from the box."

Owen took out the card and began to read the questions aloud. "How have I crucified my flesh today and given evidence of a Spirit-controlled life? Number two, How have I sought to serve my spouse today, automatically or intentionally?"

"These are the two questions I want you to ask as you journey through the green. Your verses for the next couple of weeks are Ephesians 5:18-21. Memorize these verses. Your prayer goals in the morning are on the other card."

Owen took the card and read the goals audibly. "I will seek to be filled with the Spirit of God today. Number two, I will seek to serve my spouse today."

"Okay, you have it. Begin in the morning with your prayer goals, memorize your verses, end the day with your journal questions, take two aspirin, and call me in the morning." Pastor Schaeffer said laughing. "Oh yeah, don't forget we will be having supper at our house a week from Thursday."

"I am bringing dessert, right?" Norah asked.

"That's right. I love chocolate cake by the way. Can you bring enough for six? We have another couple who will be joining us."

"That's no problem," Norah responded with curiosity.

After they prayed together, Pastor Schaeffer lead them to the door saying, "See you in a few days. Now it's time for the mystery appointment."

CHAPTER THREE

"T he weekend is finally here!" Owen shouted as he entered the door of their home after a long week at work. The children came running to hug him.

"How was your day?" Norah asked as she picked up toys in the living room.

"It was okay. We were crazy busy today, but I think we got everything knocked out. How was your day?"

"It has been wild. The phone has been ringing off the hook, the kids have been fighting and making messes. I spent thirty minutes cleaning off the bedroom wall where they decided it would be fun to draw pictures of mommy and daddy with a pencil." Norah looked at the children with disappointment.

"Have you guys been giving Mommy a hard time today?" He asked the children while they were hugging on his leg. "Well, I have some great news for this exhausted Mom." Owen reached into his back pocket and pulled out an envelope.

"Did you win the lottery?"

"Of course not. Here, take a look," Owen said as he handed her the sealed envelope.

"Are you kidding me?" Norah asked.

"Nope. And you have only about thirty minutes to get ready."

"What about the kids?"

"I have pizza coming in a few minutes and a movie in the truck for us to watch. I went ahead and set the GPS for you in the van so you can locate the spot."

"Are you kidding me?" Norah stood in astonishment.

"Well, you better get ready. They will be expecting you in thirty minutes. Oh yeah, there is a 'number 2' from McDonald's in the car seat, too. I figured you needed to eat supper."

"Are you kidding me?" That was pretty much the only response Norah could muster up. About that time the door bell rang.

"Pizza is here! Right on time . . . that's a first." Owen went to the door to get the pizza while Norah hurried to put on her shoes.

After setting the table with paper plates and pouring cups of apple juice, Norah came into the kitchen with her sweat clothes on. "Thank you so much. You don't know how much this means to me."

"Go and relax. You deserve it."

Norah got in the van and heard the GPS talk to her. "Continue driving to the highlighted route." Her estimated arrival time was fifteen minutes. As she pulled out of the drive she reached over for her "number 2" from McDonald's and began to eat. "I can't believe he did this. I could get used to marriage in the green."

Fourteen minutes later the GPS spoke up again, "You have arrived at 1515 Lander Pointe Drive." She wiped her mouth as she pulled into a parking space. She looked up at the red highlighted letters hanging over the entrance: Wild Clover Seed Massage. She had heard about this place from some of her friends, but never landed a visit.

As she came to the entrance, the door was opened by a greeter. "Welcome to Wild Clover Seed Massage. May I have your first name?"

"Norah."

"Norah, we have been expecting you. Your husband made this appointment three days ago. If you will just enter into changing room number three and get ready, our finest masseuse will call for you shortly."

She stepped into the changing room to find a fluffy white robe with the letters WCS embroidered on the pocket of the robe. Looking at the floor, she spotted a pair of brand new slippers with memory foam. She quickly put on her robe and slipped into her slippers. However, with her right foot she felt a sheet of paper. She reached down to remove it and found a small envelope with her name written on the outside. She quickly opened it up and read, "Norah, I deeply love you."

She wiped a tear from her eye as she exited the changing room. "I can't believe what's happening to me right now." She thought.

"Well, Mrs. Norah, are you ready?"

"You must be the masseuse."

"That's right. Your husband has seen fit to give you the royal treatment this evening. You will be experiencing a Swedish message designed to bring you to a state of perfect relaxation. So I don't want you to feel like you need to say a word. You simply lie here on the table and enjoy the next hour."

The sixty minutes of comfort put Norah in a dream-like state. She drifted away into complete relaxation until she heard, "Your massage is complete; you may return to your changing room."

After experiencing the best massage she had ever had in her life, Norah floated back to her changing room. She changed back into her sweat clothes and opened the door. Walking over to the front desk, she heard the voice of the greeter, "Don't forget your robe and slippers." The greeter walked over to the changing room and brought them out. After neatly folding the robe and putting the slippers into a box, she reached beneath the front desk and handed Norah a basket.

"What is this?"

"This comes with the royal treatment massage. You have Wild Clover Seed's best soaps, bath salts, a couple of scented candles, and other bath accessories."

Walking around to the desk with the box in her hand, the greeter said, "Let me help you get all of this to your van." She opened the door for Norah and followed her to her car. "Your husband is either in deep trouble or deeply in love."

"It's love!" Norah said happily. "Thank you so much," Norah responded as she put the box in the back seat along with the basket.

"We hope you visit us again soon."

"Me, too!"

Norah pulled out of the parking lot on her way home with a mixture of wonder and relaxation. Fifteen minutes later she pulled into the driveway. Walking into a silent house she saw Owen sitting on the sofa with his Bible and journal out. "Well, how was it?"

Norah couldn't even speak. She walked over to where Owen was sitting and wrapped her arms around him. "Are you crying?" whispered Owen.

"That is the sweetest thing you have ever done for me." She leaned in and gave him a kiss.

She stood up and said, "Let me go get the stuff they gave me."

Walking into the room with the basket, robe, and slippers she said, "Look at all of this stuff."

"Well, looks like you need to take a bath. I know it's extremely cheesy, but I just finished running the hot water for you. I asked the massage place to call me when you started home. So go relax some more."

Norah grinned at the thought of more relaxation. After another hug, she walked into the bathroom. The water was steaming and the mirrors were half-way fogged. Sitting next to the bath tub was a bowl of fresh fruit and a glass of cranberry juice. She sank into the tub and soaked for thirty minutes.

Meanwhile, Owen was studying the Scripture and writing in his journal. "How have I crucified my flesh today? How have I served my spouse today?" As a prayer to the Lord he wrote:

Lord,

I always felt it would be over my dead body that I would spend money like I did tonight for Norah. So I assume I am a dead man. Thank You for blessing me with a wife who has done so much to raise our children and care for our home. Help me to build her up and lift her up. I ask You to help me make You my greatest treasure in life.

I have sought to serve Norah intentionally today. I hope I haven't set the bar too high. Help me to learn how to serve her automatically.

As he closed the journal and put it on the coffee table; Norah walked in wearing her new robe and slippers. "You coming to bed? I'm ready for you."

CHAPTER FOUR

S he balled up her third sheet of paper and threw it in the garbage. The children were down for their afternoon naps while she was hard at work. "I hope he doesn't think I am doing this just because we have been going through counseling." Norah was wrestling in her mind with whether or not she should write a note to Owen to encourage and build him up. She often got intimidated by Owen's intelligence without even knowing it. She was so concerned about what he would say or what he would think. Fighting through her insecurities, Norah began her fourth draft.

Owen,

Out of all the years we have been married, I have realized something about myself. I have not expressed any gratitude to you. God has allowed me to see over the past couple of weeks what a blessing you are to our family. You really are God's gift to me.

When we were engaged, I received a book about marriage as a gift. I remember reading that the wife desires for her husband to be a provider and a protector. When the wife notices her husband displaying these attributes, she is to let him know.

Well I want to let you know. I don't worry about whether or not you are going to provide for us or protect us. Your work ethic is by far one of the greatest I have ever seen. I am overwhelmed with how much you accomplish in such a short amount of time. We never go without. I know this is because of your hard work.

You are an amazing husband. Not only do the children look up to you...but so do I. You are a great provider. I love you.

Now as far a protector is concerned. . . I know you haven't fought off enemies on the home front or anything. However, I do remember that one time when we found out a mouse was in the house. You went straight to the store and got all the necessary equipment to get rid of it. Owen, you saved us from the mouse. You are my protector.

All kidding aside, you may not realize it, but you are protecting us from an enemy. Your spiritual growth over the past several weeks has been absolutely phenomenal. Ever since we started praying together, studying our Bibles and even journaling, I have sensed a peace in our home. The strain and tension has been removed. I am thanking God that He has used you to begin protecting our home from the onslaught of our greatest enemy, the devil.

I wanted to write you this short letter just to let you know how much I love and respect you.

Norah

"Well, this is it," she thought to herself. "Now, how am I going to get this into his hands?" Norah wanted Owen to be alone when he read the note. After much thought, she came up with a great plan. Just then, the telephone rang.

"Hello."

"Hey, Babe, what you doing?"

"Nothing," Norah said quickly not wanting Owen to know she had been writing him a letter. "Just picking up around the house."

"Well, I was hoping I could home a little early today, but it looks like I might be about an hour late."

"That's fine. I'll have food on the table for you."

"Thanks, I love you," Owen said as someone in the office interrupted him with another phone call. "Got to go. I'll see you in a few."

"I love you, too."

Norah got up and found some scotch tape to carry out her plan with the note. After securing everything in the living room, Norah began working on supper. She was going to prepare one of Owen's favorites: Grandma's famous lasagna. After a couple of hours of preparation, Norah put the lasagna in the oven.

Time seemed to fly by as she set the table for the family. Owen came walking into the house and received his usual greeting from the kids. "Do I smell lasagna?" Owen looked at the table that was already set.

"It's Grandma's recipe."

"You know that is my favorite meal."

They all sat around the table and Norah began to dish out the lasagna. She began by using a large spoon that stopped about halfway down into the lasagna. She applied a little pressure, but still no progress.

"Hold on just a minute, let me get a knife." Norah opened the drawer in the kitchen and hoped she had not accidentally burned the lasagna. As soon as she cut into the lasagna with the knife, she confirmed the unfortunate reality. She tried her best to mask the loud crunching sound as she dragged the knife back and forth.

"I don't think this is Grandma's recipe," Owen said picking up the pan and looking at the bottom. "You burned it! Good grief, Norah, it's a wonder you didn't set the house on fire. We can't eat this stuff."

"I don't know what happened," Norah sighed.

"I had my heart set on that lasagna ever since I smelled it. What are we going to eat now?" Owen asked in a disappointing and disapproving tone.

"Well, I don't know, Owen. Did you bring anything?" Norah quickly retorted.

"Of course not. That's your job," Owen blurted out.

Norah was just about to retort when she remembered what she read early that morning. "I will seek to be filled with the Holy Spirit."

"Owen, if I were not submitting to the Holy Spirit right now, I would let you have it. But since I am submitting to the Spirit, I will let you have a peanut butter and jelly sandwich." Norah, dumped the burned lasagna into the trash and got the jelly out of the refrigerator.

"I'm sorry. I don't know why I acted like that." Owen stood up and walked behind Norah who was now spreading peanut butter on some bread. Wrapping his arms around her he asked, "Do you forgive me?"

"The Holy Spirit does," Norah said.

"You have to admit. . . that was pretty funny."

"You wouldn't be laughing if you had spent two hours of your life in this kitchen trying to put together a meal."

"I know, I know. I should have kept my mouth shut. Tell you what. . . I'll put the jelly on the bread."

That night Norah sat down with her green questions and her notebook. She had memorized the Scripture pretty easily and decided to write it out word for word in her journal. Then she began to write:

Lord,

I sought to crucify my flesh today, that is, the old Norah. I know that my typical response to Owen's little escapade at the dinner table could have turned into a week long fight. My first instinct was to really give him a piece of mind, and then throw the lasagna in his face. But, God, thank You for allowing me to recognize my old life and allow You to live through me at that point.

I still struggle a great deal with this concept of being controlled by You. It seems the old life continues to rule and take control. In fact, I am still seeking to not allow bitterness to take root in my heart over the little things. I need Your strength.

My prayer tonight is that Owen is greatly encouraged by the letter I wrote. I also trust You will help him find it.

Meanwhile, in the living room Owen was searching for the remote control. He finally found it hiding between the cushions of the couch. "What's this?" He asked as he picked up the remote with a piece of paper taped to it. He quickly opened it up and began to read Norah's letter.

As his eyes skimmed every line he was overcome by what Norah had said. "I never knew she was proud of me." He thought to himself as he was greatly encouraged. He laughed about the mouse incident, recalling how scared he was at that moment. "If she only knew…"

Owen took the letter and put it in his journal. He looked at the questions for the evening. He couldn't take his eyes off question number one, "How have I crucified my flesh today and given evidence of a Spirit-controlled life?" He began to write.

Lord,

I really blew it tonight. I let my flesh get the better of me. The old Owen came alive. I could sense that every word leaving my mouth tonight stunk. But, thankfully I didn't let it stop there. I asked Norah to forgive me. So now, Lord, I am asking You to forgive me.

Father, enable me to put to death the selfish desire to speak words that are unwholesome and fill me with the Holy Spirit. I want to build Norah up, not tear her down.

Also, I am so grateful for Norah. You have blessed me with a good wife. We both have our faults, but I sense You are changing us.

CHAPTER FIVE

"I guess that is the car of the other couple who is supposed to be here," Owen commented as he pulled into the Pastor's driveway. "They must be loaded. That's one of those new Hybrid Lexuses I was reading about the other day."

"I wonder if our meeting with them will be awkward?" Norah questioned, holding the miniature chocolate cakes in her lap. The inside of the truck smelled like a bakery. Owen tried to talk Norah into letting him take a quick bite. However, she refused while making a joke about his "flesh" coming alive.

"I'm sure Pastor Schaeffer will keep it light. We probably won't spend that much time talking about our marriage or anything."

As they rang the doorbell, both Norah and Owen could see the new couple through the window. "They look pretty 'well off,' " Owen commented.

The door swung open with Pastor Schaeffer giving a huge welcome. "And here they are…one of my favorite married couples in the world. He gave Norah a half hug while shaking Owen's hand. "How are you doing?"

"Great." Owen responded.

"Wait a minute, Norah. Do I smell chocolate?" Pastor was eyeballing the dessert dish.

"You sure do. I made it just for you. I hope you like it."

"I am sure he will." Addison came into the room and hugged Norah while taking the dish from her hand. "I need to put this up and out of Schaeffer's reach." Addison made her way back to the kitchen to put the final touches on the table.

"Come on over here and let me introduce you to some of my new friends," Pastor Schaeffer said. "This is Titus and MaLeah."

Owen quickly stuck out his hand to greet Titus. "Good to meet you. I'm Owen and this is my wife, Norah."

"It's great to meet you as well," Titus said.

"Tell me, how did you get stuck with this guy?" Owen laughed pointing at Pastor.

"Well, Pastor Schaeffer started a Bible Study in our office not long ago. He and I began to talk, and before I knew it, I had accepted an invite to his home. This is the first time MaLeah and I have ever eaten with a preacher."

"That is hilarious!" Norah commented. "The first time we came over here, Owen and I were in the same position."

"Yeah, I was scared to death," Owen chimed in. "I thought the house might fall in on me when God saw me walk into such a 'holy home.' "

"We will let you in on a little secret," Norah said leaning in close to MaLeah and Titus, "They really are normal people."

"Let's eat!" Addison said from the kitchen.

They all made their way back into the kitchen and sat down. Titus grabbed a french fry from his plate and quickly put it into his mouth. "I love steak fries." MaLeah kicked him under the table knowing they probably said the blessing before they ate. She was embarrassed.

"I'm glad you do," Addison said, "We have plenty of them, so eat up."

"We are so glad you were able to make it tonight." Pastor Schaeffer said in a genuine tone. "Let's say a word of prayer and dig in."

Titus and MaLeah followed the others and bowed their heads and closed their eyes. Pastor Schaeffer prayed, "Lord, thank You for allowing us to have such good friends. We also thank You for the food. In Jesus name, AMEN."

As they began to eat, Owen started the conversation. "So, Titus, what do you do?"

"I work with the Cillian and Company Branding Agency. I am the Senior Vice President of Merchandise Branding."

"Wow, that's pretty good. You enjoy working there?" Owen kept the conversation going as he cut into his steak.

"Well, I do okay. I worked my way up from the bottom of the totem pole. There were some other jobs I probably would have liked more. You know, less stress and responsibility. Now I manage twenty-five branding agents and oversee about two hundred jobs a month. But the pay is good. Not only do I get paid a ton of money, but the company's finance division helps each employee with their financial portfolio. So if anything, the security is there."

Owen listened intently to Titus go on for another five minutes about how much money he got paid. "This guy sure thinks a lot of himself," Owen thought.

"So where do you guys live?" Norah asked MaLeah.

"We just moved, actually."

"That's great," Norah smiled, "I love the feel of a new house."

"It's good. It's just hard trying to decorate all those rooms. We live on the golf course just outside of town. Our master suite has a remarkable view of the ninth hole. The ninth hole is surrounded by a pond with a beautiful bridge leading to the green. When I saw that view, I knew that house was to die for."

"Well, congratulations to both of you." Norah said wanting to change the subject. She couldn't believe how prideful the two were being about their lives. "Pastor Schaeffer, tell us how you got started doing a Bible Study at Titus's office."

"It is so interesting. You know Bill who sits on the third row of church every Sunday?" Owen and Norah nodded in agreement. "He works down at Titus's office and asked me if I would come in for a prayer breakfast once a week. We started it about four weeks ago. I do a short devotion, and then we all pray together."

"I came for the first time about three weeks ago and really enjoyed it," Titus said.

"Well, that's good," Owen said. "Where do you go to church?"

"Oh, we don't," Titus responded with a very short answer.

"You should come to our church. We absolutely love it there." Norah said with excitement.

"Yeah, and Pastor Schaeffer's sermons aren't always boring." Owen said laughing.

"Addison and I love our church, too. The people there are great, and we have the joy of serving people like Norah and Owen. But you know, while church is important, that's not the most important thing in life." Pastor Schaeffer said bringing a silence to the room. "The most important reality in a person's life is that they come into a personal relationship with Jesus Christ." Pastor Schaeffer looked toward Norah. "Norah, tell us how you came to personally know Jesus Christ."

Norah almost spit her tea out of her mouth, "You want me to tell my story?"

"Yeah," Addison encouraged her, "I don't think I ever heard the story."

"Well, okay. I'll share." Norah cleared her throat and took another drink, wondering how to begin. "I guess I'll start from the beginning. My mother and father were great people, but they were didn't go to church. In fact, neither of them ever told me anything about Jesus. Don't get me wrong; they loved me and took great care of me growing up.

"But during my junior year of high school, a good friend of mine invited me to her church. They were having some sort of a big night with some band I had never heard of. I remember asking her if there was going to be some guy teaching that I would have to listen to. She told me there would be, but he was a great speaker. I gave in and went that night. The band was okay; I wouldn't buy a CD or anything, but what got my attention was how everyone was singing along with them. They were singing songs about Jesus and even singing to Jesus.

"That was pretty weird for me. I remember while they were singing, I had this overwhelming sense of emptiness and even guilt. I had felt it before, but ignored it. But on that night, I couldn't make it go away. Then the speaker got up and the first words out of his mouth were, 'Do you ever feel empty inside? Do you ever feel a sense of guilt in your life?'

"I'll never forget it. It was as if everyone in that room disappeared and for the next twenty or thirty minutes the speaker was talking just to me. He explained how we are all born separated from God. The emptiness we have inside is due to the fact that we have no relationship with Jesus Christ. We have sinned against God and deserve the wrath of God to be poured out upon us. This kind of made me a bit nervous and even caused me to be somewhat disillusioned and even defensive.

"How could a loving God pour out wrath on me? I was a pretty decent person. I made good grades and obeyed my parents. I didn't hang out with the party crowd. I listed off all the good things I could think of in my mind. However, the list was shattered when the speaker said, 'The Bible explains that all our good works are like filthy rags in the sight of God.' *Filthy rags*?

"Then the speaker went on to say that God displayed His love by sending Jesus, His Son, to die on the cross for my sin. Then he made the statement that God treated Jesus on the cross as if he had committed all of my sin. I had never known any love like this. A love with no conditions. . .this was new to me. Then he spoke about how Jesus was resurrected and now offers all people new life. He cleanses you from your sin and comes into a personal relationship with you. Well, long story short, that night I asked Jesus to forgive me of my sin and be the Lord of my life."

MaLeah paid very close attention to Norah as she spoke. She identified with Norah's emptiness and guilt. In fact, she was amazed at the fact that to everyone else it seemed she had everything this life could offer. Yet, she still felt like something was missing. Titus, on the other hand, pretty much tried to ignore what Norah was sharing. He always felt that religion was just a crutch that people who couldn't handle the real life leaned on.

"Norah, that is a great testimony," Addison replied. "We need to get you to share that in church one Sunday."

"That's a great idea, Addi!" Pastor said enthusiastically.

"Wait a minute now. Sharing in front of five people made me nervous. I can't imagine what it would be like to be in front of the entire church," Norah replied anxiously.

"You could do it," Owen said with an encouraging tone. Norah looked at him like he had lost his mind.

"You see church is important because it helps you grow in your relationship with Jesus." Owen could feel Pastor Schaeffer's eyes looking at him. "Owen, why don't you tell us how God has used the congregation to help you grow in your relationship with Christ?"

"I had a feeling you would ask me to share something. Well, the most recent way God has worked on my life is showing me the importance of marriage. You don't know this," Owen said looking at Titus and MaLeah, "but recently Norah and I were on the verge of divorce. Our lives were unfocused to say the least, and we were both destroying our marriage. We were selfish, inconsiderate, and just plain miserable.

"Norah and I finally agreed to talk with Pastor Schaeffer about our struggles. This was our last effort before calling it quits. We sat in his office like a couple of spoiled brats. In fact, Norah and I have talked about how ridiculous we must have looked to Pastor. Anyway, Pastor began to tell us that our marriage was in the red and we needed to be in the yellow. Then he took us on a journey through the colors, and now we are in the green! I am spending time reading the Word of God every day, putting to death my old way of living and thinking, and really focusing on getting to know more of Jesus. God has used our Pastor to cause us to grow closer to Jesus and, as a result, closer to one another."

"Wait a minute," Titus interrupted. "Your marriage was in the red? What are you talking about?"

"Well Pastor Schaeffer has given four colors to describe marriages. The red is the worst. That's where we were. Then he systematically leads the couple from red to yellow, yellow to green, and green to blue. Of course, we have no clue what blue is all about. Like I said, we are in the green."

MaLeah thought to herself about their marriage. "I wonder if our marriage is in the red?"

"MaLeah," Norah broke her concentration, "did you grow up in church?"

"Kind of. We went to Catholic Mass every year for Christmas. That was more of a family tradition. We were never serious about it. But after hearing you talk, I would love to visit your church one Sunday."

Titus felt his heart stop, "What does she mean--visit one Sunday." He spoke up, "Well, I have always felt religion was a crutch. I don't mind people being religious. It doesn't bother me. I just don't want people pushing their ideas on me."

"So you think you will visit with us this Sunday?" Addison questioned.

"We'll see," Titus said trying to think of an excuse. "I don't think we can this week. We have a lunch appointment with some friends Sunday."

"No, honey, that's Saturday." MaLeah said ruining his excuse. "I don't think we have anything going on Sunday."

"She knows her calendar," Titus said wishing she would stop talking. "Sunday it is. . . what time?"

"We meet at eleven o' clock," said Owen. "You better put some of those fries in your pocket because Pastor Schaeffer is long-winded. We will meet you in the front. You can sit with us."

After a few more minutes of conversation and Norah's wonderful dessert, everyone parted company. When the door was shut, Pastor Schaeffer and Addison gave one another a high five. "It worked!" Addison said doing a little dance in the foyer.

"I can't believe how well Norah did. I started to ask Owen to share, but for some reason I asked Norah."

"Well, that was just God. While she was sharing I was praying hard for MaLeah. God heard my prayer, too. Did you notice how much she wanted to come to church Sunday?"

"Yeah, and I love how she totally ruined Titus's excuse. He knew they weren't having lunch with some friends on Sunday. I bet he is letting her have it right now in that Hybrid Lexus." Addison and Schaeffer bowed together and prayed for Titus, MaLeah, Owen, and Norah.

CHAPTER SIX

"I never dreamed that would happen to us." Norah responded out of disbelief.

"I know." Pastor put you on the spot, didn't he?" Owen responded with a smile. "But I'll have to admit, you did an awesome job!" Owen responded realizing his words were building up his wife. "In fact, I know you are scared to death about speaking in front of people, but there are tons of people who need to hear your story."

"Really," Norah said with a bit of insecurity. "Did my story make sense? I felt like I was all over the place."

"You weren't all over the place," Owen responded recalling what she shared. "The more you spoke, the more I sensed God was really using you."

"I wonder if Pastor knew they were unchurched. . ."

"In our short time with Pastor Schaeffer, I would say he definitely knew. He seems to always have a goal in mind with every meeting."

"You really sensed God working?" Norah asked.

"Didn't you see the look on MaLeah's face as you spoke? She seemed to identify with you."

"I kept noticing that Titus was trying hard not to pay attention to me. He was eating that steak like it was trying to go somewhere."

"No, he heard every word you said. The problem with him is that he doesn't think he needs a relationship with Jesus," Owen stated firmly. "But he will figure it out soon enough. I can only imagine what Pastor Schaeffer is going to preach on this Sunday."

"I know. We really need to pray for God to open their hearts to the truth of who He is this Sunday."

They pulled into the driveway of their home and Norah went in to put the children to bed. Owen went straight to his Bible, questions, and journal. He picked up his pen and began to write:

Lord,

It was truly amazing to see Norah share how she came to know you personally. I thank You for a wife who has a relationship with You and is unashamed of it. I also thank You for giving me the right words of encouragement for her. I do pray You'll give her the opportunity to share her story with our congregation very soon.

Also, I see how You are shaping Norah and me at the same time. I can't believe we had a conversation about someone's relationship to Christ this evening. We have never done that before. You have truly worked in our marriage, and for that I am truly grateful.

I pray You would give me the courage this evening to pray with Norah about Titus and MaLeah. Also, help us as we get prepared for this Sunday.

"Check this out!" Norah yelled from the computer room. "We just got an e-mail from Pastor Schaeffer." Owen got up from his time alone with the Lord and entered the computer room.

"Well, what does it say?"

Norah began to read the e-mail aloud, "Norah and Owen, it is evident you are in the green. I can see it. In fact, I am confident you are ready to explore the ocean 'blue'. Thanks so much for all you did tonight. Norah, your story was remarkable. I love to hear how God gets people's attention and changes their lives. Owen, you did a great job sharing about how God has changed your marriage. I want you to come to church thirty minutes early this Sunday. Bring the children; Addi said she would watch them while we talk for a moment. And don't forget to pray for Titus and MaLeah. See you soon."

"We are ready for the blue?" Owen asked aloud. "We have been in the green for such a short time. I think we need to hang out in the green a bit longer."

"What? Are you scared?" Norah asked Owen playfully pushing him in the stomach.

"No, I'm not scared. I just don't want us to rush it."

"Pastor Schaeffer hasn't steered us wrong yet. I'm sure we will talk some more about the green Sunday before we jump into the blue."

"I guess you're right." Owen said realizing they needed to pray for Titus and MaLeah. "Well I suppose we need to pray for them."

"All right. Let me do my evening questions first and then we can pray."

"No, let's pray now while I have the courage. I'll pray for Titus and you pray for MaLeah."

"Sounds good to me." Norah replied as she reached out for Owen's hand.

Owen began the prayer. "Lord, You have truly changed Norah and me. If You can take a marriage doomed for failure and change it by Your power, we are confident You can change Titus and MaLeah. I pray for Titus tonight. I ask that you would cause Norah's story of how she came to know You to play over and over in his mind. I ask that You would cause him to lose sleep over it tonight. I also pray You would give Pastor Schaeffer the right words for Sunday morning. Use him to preach the message of Jesus to their hearts. I pray Titus would come to know You personally, not as a religious crutch, but as the remarkable Savior. Amen."

Norah felt a little squeeze of her hand indicating to her that it was her turn to pray. "Lord, thank You for Owen. You gave him the right words to speak tonight to Titus and MaLeah both. I really think You are working on their hearts. I ask that You knock on the door of MaLeah's heart and cause her to run to You. I pray like Owen did that You wouldn't let MaLeah sleep well until she comes to You. As Pastor Schaeffer delivers Your message Sunday, I pray that MaLeah feels like she is the only one in the room. Do a great work in her heart as You have done a great work in my heart. Amen."

After they prayed Norah, asked, "Can I go do my homework now?"

"Of course you can. I have already done mine, so I am going to go ahead and get in the bed." He leaned over and gave Norah a kiss and said, "I love you."

"I love you, too." Norah said realizing simultaneously that Owen really did love her. She went to the kitchen and got a cup of decaffeinated coffee to drink. She knew if she drank regular coffee she would never be able to sleep. She was already hyped up after the night's events anyway. Sitting down she opened her Bible. While she was memorizing the Scripture from the Green card, she remembered a story from Sunday School about a potter and some clay. She looked in the index of her Bible and was directed to Jeremiah 18.

She read the first few verses:

The Word which came to Jeremiah from the Lord saying, "Arise and go down to the potter's house, and there I will announce My words to you." Then I went down to the potter's house, and there he was, making something on the wheel. But the vessel that he was making of clay was spoiled in the hand of the potter; so he remade it into another vessel, as it pleased the potter to make."—Jeremiah 18:1-4

As she read the verses she could imagine the potter working on the clay. She pictured the potter's ill-formed and useless bowl. Then it hit her: that was her marriage. Her marriage was spoiled by outside influences, internal sins, and so much more. But God, rich in His mercy, chose to reshape the bowl, her marriage. He had made her marriage into a new vessel. Norah continued to read the chapter to find that the vessel was actually the house of Israel. God was going to break their pride and reshape them. Again she thought, "That is exactly what God has done for us. He broke us and then reshaped us." After a time of prayer she began to look at her questions on the green card. She then began to write:

Dear Lord,

My flesh must have been dead today. The old Norah would have never shared with complete strangers how she came to know You personally. But You gave me the words to speak, and for that I am thankful.

Also, I would typically have been embarrassed to hear Owen say anything spiritual to a group of people. Especially when I knew he wasn't living a spiritual life at home. But, Lord, I was extremely proud of Owen tonight. I have seen a massive change in his life. We have come such a long way in such a short time: that is Your power at work. Thank You.

I see our marriage as being reshaped now. We want to be a vessel for Your use. Cleanse us and make us holy. Take our lives and use us for Your purposes. Amen.

Norah closed up her Bible and journal and headed off to bed. She turned her body towards Owen and fell into a restful sleep.

CHAPTER SEVEN

S unday came in a hurry. After rushing the children into the van, half dressed, they sped to the church. There were only a few cars in the parking lot that early. However, they saw Pastor Schaeffer's car, and knew he was waiting for them. Addison was watching out for them from the front foyer of the church. She came out to greet them and help get the children.

"Good morning!" She said with a huge smile as Norah opened the van door.

"Good morning to you. We got here as quickly as we could. I hope they both have their shoes on." Norah said with a sigh of relief.

"They do. I see all of their shoes. I'll take them to the children's play area inside. Schaeffer is waiting for you in the office, so you go ahead."

Owen and Norah headed for the front door of the church while Addison took the children. "We aren't late, are we?" Owen asked looking at his watch.

"Perfect timing," Pastor Schaeffer said peeping down the hall at them. "You are thirty minutes early for church. Right on time. Come on in to my office."

"Today is the big day!" Norah said with excitement in her voice. She had been praying for Titus and MaLeah all morning.

"What do you mean, big day?" Pastor Schaeffer asked knowing full well what she was thinking about.

"Titus and MaLeah are coming today, right?" Owen asked.

"I called them last night just to remind them, and they said they would be here at about ten till eleven. I told them you would meet them in the front foyer."

"Perfect," said Norah, "and, Pastor, you better preach a good sermon."

"No pressure," Owen said. "But don't blow this one." They all laughed together as they sat down in their usual spots in Pastor's office.

"I am so proud of both of you. Addi and I have been so excited to see you both growing closer to Jesus and to one another."

"Well we would still be in the red if it weren't for you." Owen said with appreciation in his voice.

"You know the old saying: 'You can lead a horse to water, but you can't make him drink.' All I did was lead you to the water. You both chose to drink."

"Are you calling me a horse?" Norah said laughing.

"I love hanging out with you. Ya'll are so much fun."

"Are we ready for the blue?" Owen asked a little nervous about what the blue might have in store.

"I want you in the green until this Thursday," Pastor Schaeffer said.

"Oh, I thought you were going to take us to blue today."

"No, not today."

"Then why did we meet so early?" Owen asked.

"One reason: to pray."

"Okay, what are we praying for this morning?" Norah asked.

"I want you both to spend time praying for Titus and MaLeah."

"We can do that. No problem." Owen said with confidence. "What are you preaching on today?"

"The title of my message is "Pockets with Holes in Them." You know I have been preaching a series on the Minor Prophets, and today we look at the message of Haggai. Haggai was speaking to a group of people whose priorities were out of whack. They had turned their backs on God's house and had begun to live for themselves. They were putting their money into pockets with holes in them. In essence, their lives were empty, and they were trying to fill that emptiness with temporary things. Then, as always, I will encourage people to come to Christ."

"That sounds like a good one, Pastor," Owen said. "Norah and I will pray for God's hand to be on you this morning."

Following their small group, Norah and Owen went straight to the foyer. They were a little nervous about Titus and MaLeah's coming to church that morning. Owen confirmed their fears by saying to Norah, "I'm scared to death, and I don't even know why."

"Well, good news is we really don't have to think of much to say. We just welcome them and sit down. Pastor Schaeffer does the rest."

"Oh no, is that them?" Owen said watching a Hybrid Lexus enter the parking lot.

"Sure is," Norah replied. "Just relax; you are making me nervous."

An extremely well-dressed Titus and MaLeah got out of the car. Titus wore a pin striped suit and MaLeah looked like she just stepped out of a fashion magazine. They looked toward the foyer door and saw Owen and Norah waiting for them. "There they are," Titus said. "Waiting to save our souls."

"Just hush," MaLeah said rolling her eyes. "They are just being friendly."

"Well this is it. One visit like we said; then we go back to normal life."

"What are you so scared of?" MaLeah asked closing up her purse. It had come undone as she got out of the car.

"You better tie that purse up good. I'm sure the church wants to get into it," Titus snarled.

"How is it going?" Owen asked interrupting their conversation.

"We are doing wonderful. We are so glad you invited us this morning," Titus lied through a fake smile.

"Good deal. Follow us; we saved you both a seat." Owen and Norah walked them to their seats, introducing them to several people along the way. Titus, who was normally a confident person, felt out of place as he shook hands with many strangers. On the other hand, MaLeah was pleased by the friendly welcome she received from the members of the church. The service began as soon as they sat down.

After the choir special, Pastor Schaeffer made his way to the pulpit to preach. He began by asking a very simple question, "Have you ever felt like your priorities were all out of whack? If we don't set our priorities in life correctly, our lives will be meaningless. That is what happened to the children of Israel, and God sent them a warning through the prophet Haggai. Notice with me, if you will, Haggai 1."

Pastor Schaeffer preached about how the Israelites had avoided the command of God to build the Temple and had begun to focus on themselves. He showed from Scripture that their lives were meaningless. They were gaining much, but putting their wealth into pockets with holes. It was amazing what happened during the service. Titus and MaLeah couldn't take their eyes off Pastor. He preached with power and conviction. He preached in a language which both of them understood. Following the message, Pastor

Schaeffer gave an invitation for people to come to know Christ personally. Neither MaLeah nor Titus responded. In fact, they both seemed to stand during the invitational song almost indifferent to the message.

After the closing prayer, Owen and Norah explained how thankful they were for their visit. Pastor Schaeffer came around the corner and said, "So glad you were here this morning. I know Owen and Norah took good care of you. Are you ready to go?"

"Sure are. Do you want us to just meet you there?" MaLeah asked.

"That will be perfect. It may take us about ten minutes or so, but we will be on our way. See you soon." Pastor Schaeffer said as he turned his attention to a growing line of church members wanting to speak to him.

"Where are you all going?" Owen asked.

"Pastor Schaeffer wanted to take us out to lunch. I think that was another way to get us here: promise us a free lunch."

"Whatever works," Norah said with a smile. "I guess we are not above bribery around here."

"Well, we need to go pick up our children. Thanks for coming. Hopefully we can all get together again soon." Owen said shaking Titus's hand.

After piling into the van, Norah and Owen headed toward their house. I wonder what Pastor Schaeffer and Addi are going to say to them?" Norah mused.

"No telling. I guess he will give them part two of the message," Owen said.

After lunch Owen, Norah, and the children all lay down for an afternoon nap. At about 2:30 p.m. Owen's phone buzzed, indicating a text message. He picked up his phone and saw it was from Pastor Schaeffer. He read it in disbelief. "Praise the Lord! Titus and MaLeah just accepted Christ! They are going to be baptized next Sunday."

"Norah!" Owen exclaimed pushing her arm to wake her up. "You are never going to believe this!"

"What is it?" Norah asked in an aggravated tone. "I was sleeping so good."

"They just accepted Jesus."

"Who did?" Norah asked sitting up.

"Titus and MaLeah did," Owen said wide-eyed. "I just got a text from Pastor Schaeffer."

"Give me that phone," Norah said taking the phone to read the text. "I can't believe it. Titus seemed hard as a rock this morning."

"I know."

"Well, text him back."

"What should I say? I don't know what to say when someone gets saved."

"Just type 'PTL,'" Norah said with a smile.

"What does 'PTL' stand for?"

"Praise the Lord!"

"He may not have a clue what that means," Owen said, still wondering what to put.

"Then just type out the words."

He began to type and say the words out loud, "Praise the Lord."

Another text came from Pastor Schaeffer, "See you Thursday. You will be ready for the blue."

PART IV

MARRIAGE IN THE BLUE

T he next four days for both Norah and Owen were heaven. They had memorized their verses and faithfully completed each task in the green. What seemed to keep them going was the way God moved in the lives of Titus and MaLeah. In fact, that was the subject of their conversation as they traveled to Pastor Schaeffer's office.

"I am going to ask him exactly what he said to them over lunch," Owen said. "He must know some secret about leading people to Christ."

"I know," Norah agreed. "I wonder if they actually prayed to receive Christ at the restaurant?"

"There is no way. I couldn't imagine Titus doing something like that. MaLeah maybe, but not Titus."

He put the van in park, turned to Norah, and said, "You ready to set sail?"

"What are you talking about?"

"To set sail on the ocean 'blue'."

"You have been spending too much time with Pastor Schaeffer. That was corny for sure," Norah said forcing a fake laugh.

As they opened the door to the front office, Owen curiously asked Norah, "I wonder if this will be our last meeting with Pastor?"

"I hope not. They have become our friends now. I think these counseling sessions have turned out differently than he and Addi expected."

The church secretary, Marlene, saw Owen and Norah enter and said, "Pastor Schaeffer asked me to give you this." She pushed a refrigerator sized box into the middle of the waiting area. The box was poorly wrapped with newspaper and had a huge tacky maroon bow on the top. "He said you were to open it before I could let you in."

"What in the world? That's the largest present I have ever seen," Owen commented.

"It's the largest present I have ever seen him give," Marlene said as she rushed to answer the ringing phone on her desk. Norah and Owen looked at the box for a moment. Covering the mouthpiece of the telephone, Marlene said, "Go ahead and open it. Pastor is waiting for you."

"Okay," Norah said as she began to rip the newspaper from the top of the box to the bottom. After they finished unwrapping the huge box, they opened it to find another wrapped box about half the size of the refrigerator box. They unwrapped it to find another box. They did this four times before they reached a blue box. "We found it!" Norah shouted as she held the box above her head.

"Pastor Schaeffer asked me to tell you not to open that box yet. Take that with you to his office," the secretary said as she began to pick up the newspaper and put it in the trash. "I'll clean this up. You go ahead and enjoy the blue."

As they turned to walk toward Pastor Schaeffer's office, they noticed the door was cracked. They also heard some laughing as they got closer to the door. Pastor Schaeffer had watched them opening the boxes the entire time. From the crack in the door he said, "I have never seen anyone so excited to find a blue box!"

"Were you watching us the whole time?" Owen asked as he opened the office door.

"Of course I was; I wouldn't have missed that for the world. Norah was ripping through that box like there might be gold in it."

"Well, we are dying to hear," Norah said.

"Hear what?"

"We want to know what happened at the restaurant Sunday," Owen said as he and Norah sat down.

"It was so easy. I wish every witnessing opportunity went that well."

"What did you say to them?" Norah asked.

"When we got to the table and sat down, we noticed MaLeah had been crying. She tried to hide it, but was unable to. So Addi simply asked her what was wrong. Then MaLeah began to spill her guts. She said she hadn't slept well all week. She even said Norah's story played over and over in her mind."

"You're kidding!" Norah said while looking at Owen. "We prayed for them every day. I asked the Lord to keep the story in her mind and not let her sleep well."

"He definitely answered your prayer."

"So what happened next?" Owen asked with curiosity.

"She said she wanted to know more about having a personal relationship with Jesus. So Addi began to share with her how she could. Then she asked her if she wanted to pray to receive Christ. She said, 'Yes!' We bowed our heads and MaLeah prayed from her heart one of the sweetest prayers I have ever heard. You should have seen it. She wasn't sure how to end the prayer, so she just said, 'I'm done.' We opened our eyes and MaLeah's entire demeanor changed on the spot. She had a total sense of peace."

"That is unbelievable," Owen said with excitement. "But what about Titus?"

"Titus was a hard nut to crack. Following MaLeah's prayer, I focused my attention on him. When I take someone out to eat, I typically ask them the same question. 'Tell me what stood out to you in the message today?' Titus then looked at me with a hard look. He actually made me a little nervous. I thought he was angry."

"What did he say?" Owen tried to speed up the story.

"He said, 'Did you try to put that speech together just for me?' I said, 'Of course not, why?' He continued to explain how he felt as if he were the only one in the building that morning. The title alone got him asking, 'Do my pockets have holes in them?' Then he began to explain how he had been feeling lately--as if his life were meaningless. He made a lot of money, but still felt empty. Then he practically quoted the last paragraph of the message to me. He explained how Israel had forsaken the Lord, and he concluded that was his problem as well.

"And, Norah, you will love this part; he said all he could think about was the fact that God's wrath was headed toward him. His money, job, not even his million-dollar home could stop the wrath of God. So I asked him what he believed God was asking him to do. He said, 'I need to stop trusting in temporary things and give my life to Christ. . . I think.' So I explained that was exactly what he needed to do."

"Did he pray like MaLeah?" Norah asked.

"He sure did. We bowed our heads again and then he prayed. His prayer was shorter than MaLeah's, but still heartfelt. When he finished he said the same thing as MaLeah, 'I'm done.' You should have seen him! I am telling you he looked like he was glowing. It was obvious a ton of weight had been lifted off his shoulders. You probably won't even recognize them next time you see them."

"That is amazing," Norah said, "I never knew you could have church in a restaurant."

"I can't wait to see them again. Didn't you say they were going to be baptized this Sunday?" asked Owen.

"Yeah, they will. I am actually going to see Titus tomorrow at the office to give him the final details. I want to thank both of you for being faithful to God at our house the other night. God used both of you to lead them to Christ."

Norah and Owen just sat stunned in their chairs. They were shocked that God could use them to make such an eternal impact. They recalled how only a short time ago, they were both on their way to calling it quits in their marriage. Now God was using them as His mouthpiece to speak to those without Christ.

"Now it's time for," Pastor Schaeffer took two pencils and did a drum roll on his desk and said with a stadium voice, "Marriage in the Blue."

CHAPTER TWO

P astor Schaeffer sat back in his chair and began to explain, "Most couples who come as far as you have typically teeter-tottered between green and blue. While this is not terrible, the goal is the blue. Don't get me wrong; all the principles you have learned from each color are to be continually applied to your marriage. As they are applied, you will find that blue is the next obvious step."

"Okay, so what are the descriptions for the blue?" asked Owen.

"Like the green, there are two major descriptions for a marriage in the blue. First of all, a marriage in the blue is a mission-minded couple. Secondly, a marriage in the blue is a mentor-minded couple."

Norah leaned up in her chair and asked, "What do you mean *mission-minded*? Do we have to go on a mission trip or something? I don't know if I can handle a third-world country."

"While going overseas is a mission, many in the church have a false idea about being mission-minded. The Bible explains that we are all ambassadors for Christ. We don't *go* on missions; we are *on* a mission. Every day of our lives is another day we are speaking on behalf of Heaven about the grace of Christ."

"Let's look at a few scriptures together," Pastor Schaeffer said leaning over to take his Bible from the corner of his desk. Jesus gave us clear instructions about being mission-minded in Matthew 28:19-20:

> Go therefore and make disciples of all the nations, baptizing them in the name of the Father, and the Son and the Holy Spirit, teaching them to observe all that I have commanded you; and lo, I am with you always until the end of the age.—Matthew 28:19-20

"I guess that will be our memory verse?" Owen asked.

"You are getting the hang of this, aren't you?" Pastor Schaeffer responded. "When Jesus told us to 'go,' he was using a tense form which literally means 'as you go.' As you go, make disciples. Jesus was teaching that this was to be a way of life."

"I'm with you so far," Owen said. "However, the question is _how_ do we make disciples?"

"You don't know it, but you have already been in the process of making disciples."

"What do you mean? Asked Norah. "You aren't talking about Titus and MaLeah, are you?"

"That is exactly who I am talking about. Addi and I are seeking to be a marriage that is in the blue. As a result we live to be mission-minded. When I met Titus I knew God wanted me to focus on him and his wife. That is why I have been spending time with him. Our goal was to share the Gospel with them. We met that goal the night you came over."

"That's pretty good," Owen remarked. "I knew you had a plan when we got there. I just wasn't sure what it was."

"Let me explain something God taught me a few years ago. I learned this studying the book of Ephesians. Let me first state the simple truth and then give an explanation. You ready for the simple truth?"

"Preach it!" Owen said with enthusiasm.

"The Gospel flows through relationships. Now picture a boat called 'The Gospel' flowing through the river of my marriage. Addi and I have to keep the river completely free of debris and be certain we don't build dams which would stop the flow of the Gospel through us. God wants to use our marriage as a witnessing tool for other marriages. Marriage is a picture of Jesus's relationship to the New Testament Church. You may remember, as a couple without Christ sees Addi and me, they should see a picture of Christ's love with the Church."

"I think I get it," Owen chimed in. "If we are in the red, we are keeping the Gospel from flowing through our marriage."

"That's exactly right. Think about it. When was the last time you shared with another married couple what God was doing in your life before Titus and MaLeah?"

"We didn't." Norah answered.

"That's because you had too much debris. You had built dams in your marriage which stopped you from being mission-minded. You were stopping the Gospel boat from getting through. I am confident that is why Paul ends Ephesians by explaining spiritual warfare. He writes about relationship after relationship. Then he says, 'We don't wrestle against flesh and blood.' Our enemy is the devil. So the enemy seeks to destroy relationships like marriage because he knows this will stop the flow of the Gospel."

"I have never thought about it like that," Norah said as the truth landed in her heart.

"I never did either," Pastor Schaeffer said. "Until God opened my eyes to it. Take a look in the blue box and pull out the morning prayer cards."

They took the cards and looked them over. Owen read the first one aloud, "We will seek to build a relationship with a couple in order to share Christ with them."

"When you are in the blue, this has to be a priority in your marriage. This means you have to get to know people who are without Christ," Pastor Schaeffer explained.

"So how do we build relationships with lost people?" Norah asked.

"Jesus said, 'As you go.' In other words, you both need to consider *where you go*. Think about your journey, Norah. You spend time taking your children on play dates. What about the moms who are there? Are any of them without Christ?"

"I never really thought about it," Norah shamefully admitted. "There are a couple of them who don't go to church anywhere."

"And you, Owen, as you go to work, are there any men who are without Christ? You mentioned the Christmas parties before. Sounds like there may be some couples there who are without Christ."

"That's true," Owen said looking at the floor. "I just never have thought about their eternal destination. I was too busy making fun of them."

"Look, I sense a load of guilt coming over you. That is not the point of marriage in the blue. The goal is not to coerce you into becoming mission-minded. That kind of motivation won't last. You have to view this as an opportunity God has placed before you. What I want you to do this week is pray together about who God may have already put in your path who doesn't know Him. You need to discuss this together and build a strategy into your relationship to share Jesus."

"I guess we can do it," Owen said unsurely.

"Of course you can. God doesn't ask you to do something He won't equip you to do. Besides, you have already done it. I am witness to that fact myself."

"Tell us about the mentor-minded couple," Norah said eager to learn more.

"The mentor-minded couple is pretty easy. Just as Addi and I have identified Titus and MaLeah as our mission focus, we have identified you as our mentor focus."

"Us?" Norah and Owen said at the same time.

"Yes, you. When you are in the blue, you look for marriages in the red. The goal is to progressively lead them through each color. Listen to what Paul writes in Galatians 6:1; and, yes, this is another memory verse:

Brethren, even if anyone is caught in any trespass, you who are spiritual, restore such a one in a spirit of gentleness; each one looking to yourself, so that you too will not be tempted.—Galatians 6:1

Pastor continued, "Paul says, 'restore such a one.' He is using medical language here which was also used in Greek culture to describe setting someone's broken bone.

"There are couples in our congregation who are in the red. They have broken the legs of their marriage so to speak. You are now equipped with the colors to help them walk again. That is what Addi and I did with you."

"Pastor, I am thankful for your confidence, but neither Norah nor I have any kind of counseling skills."

"I think it is pretty funny that you think I have counseling skills. I am not a counselor. The colors are just a tool to guide your discussions. Think about it; is there a couple you know that is in the red?"

"I don't think Owen and I have gotten to know anyone that well at church."

"Precisely. That's the problem with most congregations. We have not spent time getting to know one another. We will be unable to fulfill Galatians 6:1 if we don't know one another within the fellowship of believers. Again, what has kept you guys from seeing the power of the Gospel flow through your lives to mentor one another?"

"We were in the red." Norah said.

"You got it. The Gospel is God's grace for justification, declaring us righteous by faith in Christ, as well as for sanctification. Sanctification is God's gracious ability to shape and mold us into the image of His Son. However, the powerful message of the Gospel is stopped from flowing through us if we stay in the red. The Gospel is flowing through your marriage now. Now is the time to help others walk again by mentoring them. Mentoring is just building a relationship with them."

"I think it would be wise for us to carry another couple through the colors. That way it keeps the principles fresh in our minds, too." Owen said as he looked at Norah.

"Yeah, but who will we mentor?"

"I am always trying to connect people to this mentoring process. I know of more than one marriage in our church family that is in the red. One of them is in your small group."

"Who is it? Everyone in there seems to have it all together. I thought we were the only couple with problems." Owen said, wondering who Pastor Schaeffer was talking about.

"I can't tell you their names yet. I have an appointment with them tomorrow afternoon. Here is what I want to do."

"Oh no, here we go again." Owen said nervously.

"No worries. What I want to do is explain to them that they are in the red. Then encourage them to come up to you on Sunday Morning after worship and say, 'We are in the red.' All you need to do is be prepared to help them."

"What if we mess up?" Norah asked.

"Yeah, I would hate to break their arms, too." Owen said laughing.

"Here is my commitment to you. I will be available to help you, prepare you, or consult with you at any time during your mentoring of them. How does that sound?"

"You make it hard to say, 'No'." Owen said.

"Good deal. Norah read the next morning prayer focus on the blue card."

She read aloud, "We will seek to help another marriage grow."

"There you have it. Your two prayer goals: Ask God to make you a mission-minded couple and a mentor-minded couple. Your verses are from Matthew and Galatians. Now take a look at your evening questions."

Norah took the cards out and read them: "How have my spouse and I prepared to reach out to another couple with the Gospel? What marriage has God put in our path that we can help grow?"

"Think about how awesome it is going to be Sunday. We will see a couple baptized who came to faith in Christ last week, and you will have a couple to begin mentoring," Pastor Schaeffer said with gusto. "Now that is God's church!"

CHAPTER THREE

That night after the children were put to bed, Norah and Owen sat in the living room next to one another on the couch. Owen turned the television off with one touch to the remote control and began to share his heart. "I don't know about this marriage in the blue stuff."

"What do you mean?" Norah asked maneuvering herself on the couch to face Owen.

"Well I feel like we--or maybe I should just say--I feel unqualified to do what Pastor Schaeffer is asking of me."

Thinking back to the green, Norah wanted to be sensitive to Owen, but extremely encouraging at the same time. "I know how you feel. We aren't qualified. But I'll have to say I have never seen you as close to the Lord as you are right now."

"Yeah, but being close to Jesus and qualified to mentor others is two different things."

"I don't know. You help people at work all the time. Don't you kind of mentor people at work?"

"Yeah, but that is different. I know what I'm talking about at work."

"Okay. So if God asks us to do something we are uncomfortable with or something we feel unqualified for, what does that mean for us?"

"I don't know," Owen said looking at the coffee table in front of him. "I guess we need to get a counseling degree, or go to seminary, or something."

"That isn't the answer I had in mind."

"What is the answer you had in mind?" Owen shot Norah a quizzical look.

"If God asked me to do something I know I can't do, then I must trust Him to do it through me."

Owen looked at Norah, "Are you saying this is a 'trust-test'?"

"I think so. This will just be another area in our lives where we have to trust Christ to use us."

"I can't even think of any people who are without Christ right now." Owen made an excuse to try to get out of it.

"As I was putting the children to bed, I asked God to put some people on my mind who we could begin to build a relationship with. . ."

"Don't tell me He did," Owen said abruptly.

"He sure did. I meet with Peggy at the park once every two weeks. I know she doesn't have a relationship with Christ, and I am pretty sure her husband doesn't either."

Owen came back with another excuse, "What if we start to build a relationship with them, and we realize we don't like them."

"We didn't like Titus and MaLeah."

"Point taken. However, we still don't know if we will like them. What does Peggy's husband do for a living?"

"I don't have a clue. But I'm supposed to meet her Wednesday morning at the park. I'll go ahead and invite them over the house Friday night for dinner." Norah said quickly.

"Friday night! That's a little quick, isn't it?"

"Yes, but if we don't do it quickly, I'm afraid we won't do it at all. We could be in danger of just putting it off indefinitely."

"You're right," Owen said. "I hate it when you're right."

"You must be hating it a good bit then because I'm always right."

"Real funny," Owen said sarcastically. "I'm going to do my homework."

"Me, too."

Owen stayed on the couch while Norah went to the bedroom. After Norah left the room, Owen shook his head and thought, "I wanted to sail the ocean blue; I just didn't know the seas were going to be so rough."

Owen looked at his evening questions: How have my spouse and I prepared to reach out to another couple with the Gospel? What marriage has God put in our path that we can help grow? Owen began to write in his journal a prayer to the Lord.

Father,

You know my heart, so there is no use in trying to hide it. I am scared to death about what Pastor Schaeffer is asking us to do now. I really would rather just stay in the green.

Now Norah says You have put a couple in her mind: Peggy and her husband. I would like to see them come to You personally; I just don't know if I would like for You to use us to make it happen.

I'm scared. But as You taught me through Norah tonight, I need to trust You fully. So, Lord, I hate to say it, but all the pressure is on You. I am going to be obedient to the mission thing and this mentoring thing, but You are going to have to teach me and speak through me.

So give me strength to accomplish Your purposes. I don't know, but is it wrong for me to ask that You would make Peggy and her husband's schedule busy for Friday night?

Owen closed his journal and looked at his memory verses again. Norah had already finished writing in her journal and had just gotten in bed. Owen climbed in the bed next to Norah and said out loud, "I think we have lost our minds."

"It is going to be just fine."

Once again, the morning came quickly, and Norah got out of bed to spend time with the Lord. She read the first statement on the card: We will seek to build a relationship with a couple in order to share Christ with them. She began to pray, "Lord, I want You to use Owen and me to share the Gospel with Peggy and her husband. I pray their schedule is open for Friday night, and we can get together. Amen."

Owen was already off to work when Norah decided she would make a phone call. She dialed the number nervously and heard a voice on the other end, "Hello."

"Is this Peggy?"

"Yeah, how are you Norah?"

"How did you know it was me?"

"Caller I.D. It works every time. How are you?"

"I am great. Just wanted to make sure you were still planning on coming to the park tomorrow."

"I sure am. Hopefully we will be there on time this go round. I hate being late. It makes me feel like the loser mom."

"That's funny, I often gave myself that title in the past," Norah said with a nervous laugh. "Hey, Owen and I want to hang out with some people this Friday night. Do you think you and your husband--I don't think I know his name--would like to come over for dinner?"

"His name is Jake. Oh, I would love to come over, but Friday night he has some conference call with his team leader at work."

"That's too bad."

"How about Thursday night though. I know he is off then?"

"Do you need to ask him?"

"No, girl, who do you think runs this household?" Peggy said laughing through the phone.

"Thursday night it is then. How does 6:30 sound?"

"Perfect. Tell you what; let me bring a salad and some dessert."

Norah was shocked she so readily accepted an invitation. "That's great. Do you like Lasagna?"

"Love it."

"Okay then, I'll try not to burn it this time. See you tomorrow at the park."

"Sounds great. Bye."

"Bye." Norah hung up the phone and thought, "I can't wait to tell Owen." She quickly sent a text off to him which read: They can't make it Friday night.

Owen was sitting at his desk answering e-mails when his cell phone buzzed indicating an incoming text. He picked it up and saw the message from Norah. He immediately held both of his hands up in victory and said, "Thank You Lord! You have answered my prayer."

Then the phone buzzed again, indicating another message: They are coming Thursday night instead. His joy went from a ten to a zero. "I guess I should have been a little more specific in my prayer request." He took his phone and shot her a text back: PTL.

Wednesday came and Norah was headed to the park. She had focused her prayer times on Peggy and Jake. As she drove, she specifically prayed for Peggy's salvation. She and Peggy spent pretty much the entire time at the park in conversation. It wasn't a really good one because they were constantly interrupted by their children getting hurt, whining, or wanting something to eat or drink. When they left, they confirmed their dinner date and the directions to get to Norah's house.

On Thursday morning Norah was checking the family e-mail. There was an e-mail from Pastor Schaeffer.

Hope you are having a great week. I have been praying for God to put someone in your path you could build a relationship with to share the Gospel. Things are great on this end. You will have a couple come to you in church Sunday and say, "We are in the red." That's the couple you will be mentoring. They already know the plan, so the stage is set.

I also have another great idea. Norah, this Sunday I want you to share your story with the congregation. Just do exactly what you did at the dinner table the other night, and it will be perfect. Don't worry about it all week though. Just come in, and I'll call you up when it's your turn.

See you Sunday. Your friend,

Pastor Schaeffer.

"He must be trying to make me crazy," Norah said running her hand through her hair. Owen was walking past the room and heard her.

"Who is trying to make you crazy?"

"Pastor Schaeffer. He wants me to share my testimony Sunday morning. Can you believe it?

"Sure I can. They both talked about your doing it. You might as well do it now, or you will just keep putting it off."

"You are starting to get on my nerves," Norah said.

"I'll be praying for you. I know God answers my prayers. You will do just fine. I have to go now. I'll be home early tonight ready to hang out with Peggy and John."

"It's Jake. Don't call him John tonight!"

"I won't. I'm just messing with you anyway," Owen said as he walked out the door. "Love you."

CHAPTER FOUR

The doorbell rang. "They're here!" Owen announced as he went to open the front door. Norah ran to pick up a few unnoticed toys off the couch. Peggy stood in front of Jake, armed with her bowl of salad and ready for the evening. Jake, on the other hand, holding the dessert felt like an uninvited guest.

"How are you doing?" Owen asked as he welcomed them into the foyer. Norah came walking around the corner and greeted Peggy with a hug. "I'm Owen," he said reaching out his hand to shake Jake's.

"I'm Jake. It's nice to meet you."

"I think our wives came up with this idea."

"Yeah, I told her it was a bit awkward for me not knowing you or Norah."

"No worries here; I felt the same way." Owen said with a quick laugh. "It will be fun. So come on in, and we can act like we have known each other for years."

The table was already set for dinner that night; the tea was poured, the bread was warm, the salad and dessert were now in place, and--most importantly--the lasagna wasn't burned. They made small talk over dinner about their kids, their jobs, and their hobbies. Jake and Owen discovered they both loved to play golf and even played at the same golf course. Norah, who had never been excited about golf, was glad it became the common ground for their conversation.

"So what's going on with you, Norah?" Peggy asked realizing she seemed a little stressed.

"What do you mean?"

"You seem a little high strung tonight. I hope our visit didn't stir you up."

"Of course not," Norah knew why she seemed preoccupied. She was scared to death about sharing her story Sunday morning in front of so many people. However, she wasn't sure if she should tell them. She didn't want to come off too churchy too quickly. "It's nothing."

"Come on, girl, you can tell me," Peggy pressed.

"Okay," Norah thought about how she could share her news without mentioning church, "I have a public speech I have to give soon, and I am scared to death."

"A public speech? I didn't know you did that kind of stuff." Peggy wouldn't give up the conversation about the public speech. "So where are you giving it?"

Owen became nervous for Norah at this point. He knew she was avoiding the whole scoop. He mentally prayed for his wife to go ahead and share.

"I am giving a public speech at church on Sunday."

"Really?" Jake joined the conversation after taking a sip of his sweet tea.

"What do you have to talk about?" Peggy asked with interest.

"I have to share my story with the church."

"Your story?" Norah felt like she was being drilled with questions. She even thought that God should have eased her in to this missionary concept.

"Yep, my story," Norah said as she took a long hard swallow.

Owen jumped in the conversation to save his drowning wife. "This Sunday she will be telling the church about the difference God has made in her life." Owen wanted to say "Jesus", but he didn't. He assumed the name God would be less abrasive.

"I can't stand giving speeches." Jake said taking the spotlight off Norah. "The last speech I gave, I fumbled over my words like a two year old trying to learn to speak."

"Jake, shut it. That's not making her feel any better. I'm sure you will do just fine." Peggy offered as a word of encouragement.

"You should come and listen," Owen invited adding greater pressure to Norah.

"We couldn't do that. Norah is already nervous; our presence would just make it worse."

Realizing she wouldn't have to share her story at the dinner table, Norah's courage picked up. "You know what?" Norah seized the opportunity. "I would actually feel better if I had some friends there to support me."

Owen sat up in his chair appreciating what his wife had just done. "That is a great idea. You come Sunday, and after church we could grab a quick bite to eat, and Jake and I can go hit nine holes." Owen loved to play golf and now saw his hobby as a tool to be used in being a missionary.

Jake hadn't played golf in about three weeks and had the fever. "I haven't been to church since I was nine years old. I'm sure it wouldn't hurt. In fact, a visit to church may be what my golf game needs." Jake accepted the invitation looking forward to golf.

"All right then," Peggy interjected. "We'll be there! Tell you what, Norah; we will sit on the front row and cheer for you during your speech." They all laughed together and the subject of the speech was over.

After dinner, while Norah and Peggy cleaned up the kitchen, Owen showed Jake his practice putting green in the garage. They took turns hitting the golf ball and talking about the nine holes they would be playing on Sunday. Once they left the house, Norah and Owen hugged one another in the foyer. "That was pretty easy," Norah said.

"I know. I think the golf idea worked."

"Yeah, I love how you scheduled yourself a day of golf around church." Norah looked at Owen to let him know he didn't get away with anything.

"Hey, Babe, somebody has to suffer for the Lord's work."

Saturday night Norah couldn't sleep. She was pacing the living room floor, repeatedly practicing her story in her mind. Owen had his golf bag packed with brand new tees and a pack of Nike golf balls. The sun seemed to come up earlier to Norah on that Sunday morning. She barely slept a wink, but found herself still wide awake, thanks to pure adrenaline.

"You ready?" Owen asked as they buckled the children in the car.

"Do I have a choice?"

As they drove into the parking lot, Owen turned around and said to the kids "Let's say a prayer for Mommy before we go in."

They all bowed their heads and Owen began, "Lord, we ask that you would give Mommy great courage as she stands up and shares today. We also pray that her story would be a great tool in leading other people to faith in You. Speak clearly to Peggy and Jake's hearts and draw them to Yourself. Also, help me to beat Jake at golf today. Amen."

Norah hit Owen on the arm playfully, "You are so bad. Thanks for the prayer though. That helped."

"You will do fine. Just be yourself."

Peggy and Jake came to church right on time. Owen met them in the foyer. "I hope you wore your lucky golf shirt today." Owen said to Jake laughing.

"It's the socks, man, the socks. I have never lost wearing these socks." Jake said lifting up his pant leg to display the PING logo.

"Oh no, PING socks. I'm in trouble."

"Where is Norah?" Peggy asked.

"She has to sit on the front row." The choir began to walk in and take their places. "They are just about to start. I saved us a spot in the middle of the church." They took their seats. Norah looked back and saw Peggy waving. She waved and said a little prayer for her.

After the choir finished their special song for that morning, Pastor Schaeffer walked out into the baptismal pool. Jake leaned over and whispered to Owen, "I didn't know you had a hot tub at church." They both laughed quietly.

"Church family," Pastor Schaeffer began, "I am so pleased to introduce to you two brand new followers of Christ. They are coming today to profess their faith in public, through baptism, the decision they made in private to accept Christ as their Savior." Pastor Schaeffer motioned with his hand for them to enter the baptismal pool. "This is Titus and Maleah Hall. God used Owen and Norah a couple of weeks ago to impact their lives for eternity. Addison and I took them to lunch, and they both prayed to receive Christ last Sunday." After Pastor Schaeffer baptized them both, the congregation stood to their feet and applauded.

From the baptismal pool, Pastor Schaeffer said, as Titus and MaLeah exited, "I have asked Norah to come share the same story with us today that she shared with MaLeah and Titus in our home. Now she is really nervous about standing in front of so many people this morning, so make her feel welcome as she comes to share." The church enthusiastically applauded as Norah made her way to the platform.

That morning God gave her an extra measure of grace. She told her story with both compassion and conviction. The congregation sat in silence as God used Norah in a way she had never been used before. Owen was awe-struck at Norah's ability to stand and speak with such confidence. His heart almost exploded with immense love for his wife. When she finished, she took her seat next to Owen. Peggy leaned over and said, "Norah, that was great!"

The service seemed to fly by; Pastor Schaeffer soon closed in prayer. As everyone stood up to leave, Jake spoke to Norah. "Norah, you are a natural. You looked like you have been giving speeches your whole life."

"Thanks. I was scared to death."

"Well, girl, you couldn't tell it." Peggy said giving her a hug.

While others walked by and thanked Norah for sharing, Owen proudly stood beside her. Brian and Linda, the most faithful Sunday School attendees in Owen and Norah's class, came up to Norah and Owen. Linda began, "Norah, your story this morning was absolutely wonderful. Thank you so much for sharing with us. You really touched me with your words."

"Thank you so much. I can't believe Pastor Schaeffer asked me to share in front of the whole church."

Brian moved in really close to Norah and Owen practically whispering, "Pastor Schaeffer told me to tell you both, we are in the red."

Owen was stunned. "How could Brian and Linda be in the red?" He thought. "They look like the happiest couple in the church."

Norah realized Owen didn't know what to say so she spoke up, "Well, we were there too, but Pastor Schaeffer led us to the Marriage Promised Land." Norah made a little joke to ease the tension.

Owen came out of his state of shock, "Tell you what. We will call you tomorrow and set up a time for ya'll to come over this week for dinner."

"That sounds good," Brian said looking at the floor a little embarrassed. "We are encouraged to know that the Marriage Promised Land is reachable."

As they walked away from Owen and Norah, Owen saw Pastor Schaeffer from across the room. He was standing there with his Bible in his left hand and a huge "thumbs up" with his right hand. After finishing his conversation with a visitor to the church, he walked over to Owen and Norah.

"Norah," Pastor Schaeffer said leaning over to give her a half-hug, "you did it! That was great. God really used you this morning!"

"Thank you so much."

"Hey, Pastor Schaeffer, I want to introduce you to a couple of our new friends." Owen waved Jake and Peggy over. "This is Jake and Peggy McDonald. Peggy and Norah know each other through our kid's play group. I just met Jake last Thursday Night. He and I are going to go hit a round of golf after lunch."

"It is so good to meet you both. Do you attend church anywhere?"

"No, I haven't been to church since I was nine years old. We came to support Norah. She was pretty scared about giving her speech this morning."

"Thanks so much for coming. I hope you come again."

"You might want to say a quick prayer for Owen this afternoon," Jake said smiling, "He might lose his religion after I beat him on the golf course."

Pastor Schaeffer laughed. "I'll pray for him."

CHAPTER FIVE

"He's a sandbagger!" Owen exclaimed as he walked through the garage door into the kitchen. He had just finished playing golf with Jake.

"Didn't do well?" Norah asked as she was sitting at the kitchen table drinking a cup of hot tea.

"The guy used to be practically a golf pro when he was in college. That was a bit of information he elected not to share last Thursday night."

"Did you have fun?"

"It was fun. He is actually a pretty cool guy. But enough about that," Owen leaned over and kissed Norah on the forehead, "You were the star at church today."

"That wasn't the point. I was trying to tell people about Jesus."

"You know what I mean. You did a fantastic job. I was so proud of you. I wanted to stand up and yell, 'That's my wife!' "

"You're so crazy."

"So, what's up with Brian and Linda?" Owen asked with a shocked look.

"I know. They were the last people I would have expected to be in the red."

"I know, I told him I would give him a call tomorrow, but I think I am going to go ahead and call him now." Owen walked over toward the phone. "Do we have their number?"

About that time the phone rang in the kitchen. Owen read the caller I.D. and said, "It's Titus!" He picked up the phone and said, "What's going on, Titus?"

"This is MaLeah."

"Oh, I'm sorry I read the caller I.D. and figured it was Titus calling. Norah and I were pumped this morning to see you guys get baptized. We tried to find you after church."

"Titus and I really appreciate you both for taking time to share with us at Pastor's house the other night. We want to return the favor. Are you free Friday night?"

"Oh no, we made plans with Jake and Peggy for Friday night."

"Were those the people sitting next to you at church?"

"Yep, Norah and I are trying to share the Gospel with them, too."

"Tell you what. I don't want to impose, but what if you just bring them with you Friday night, and we all go out. Our treat!"

"That sounds great to me. I'll run it by Jake and see what he thinks. I'm sure they would love to hang out with another couple anyway."

"Perfect. Let's meet at the steak house on First Street around seven."

"I love that place. You don't have to treat us though. We'll take care of it."

"No. We want to treat you."

"Okay, my mom taught me not to argue with women."

"Looking forward to it. See you Friday." MaLeah said as she hung up the phone.

"What did she say?" Norah asked.

"They want to take us all out to eat Friday night."

"That will be fun. I'll e-mail Peggy and let her know." Norah said taking her tea with her to the computer room.

"I'm going to call Brian."

He dialed the number, and it rang three and a half times before Linda picked up, "Hello."

"Linda, this is Owen from church."

"How are you?"

"I am great. Is Brian around?"

"Yeah, hold on just a second and I'll get him." Owen could hear Linda yelling for Brian.

"Hello."

"Brian," Owen heard Linda hang up. "This is Owen."

"Sorry we put you on the spot this morning."

"No problem. We were expecting a couple to come and let us know they were in the red anyway. To be honest though, we were shocked it was you."

"I know. This has been a long time coming. Our visit to Pastor Schaeffer was our last ditch effort to keep this marriage alive. We are on life support right now."

"Norah and I were in the same position. In fact, we were already reaching for the plug! Anyway, we can discuss that more when we get together. Is there a good time for you this week?"

"After you mentioned that to me at church, I realized our entire week is full. So I went ahead and checked the following week. Does Monday night sound okay?"

"Monday night. Yeah, man, that sounds good to me. Just plan to come over to our house around seven, and we will get started."

"Thanks, Owen, I really do appreciate it."

After hanging up the phone, Owen saw Norah walk back into the kitchen. "Peggy was online, so I just sent her an instant message. She was excited about spending time with MaLeah and Titus."

"Good deal."

"What about Brian and Linda?" Norah asked.

"They want to get together with us next Monday night."

"I thought we were going to get together this week."

"Me, too, but Brian said the first available night was Monday. So I accepted. They are going to come over for dinner."

"Do you see what's happening?" Norah asked as she took her seat back at the kitchen table.

"What?"

"We are in the blue—like, for real, in the blue."

"I know." Owen pulled out a chair and took a seat as well. "I never knew it would be so much fun."

"I never knew it would include golf."

They both laughed for a moment and then began to discuss Friday night. "You remember how Pastor Schaeffer got you to share your story in front of Titus and MaLeah the other night?"

"What do you think?" Norah exaggerated her words as she said them.

"Of course you do." Owen leaned in toward Norah putting an elbow on the table. "I have an idea."

"What is it?"

"What if we ask MaLeah or Titus to share their story with us over dinner? That way Brian and Peggy can hear the Gospel!"

"That's a great idea. So how will we get them to do it?"

"Simple. I'll just ask them about their conversation with Pastor Schaeffer. That should lead them right into their story."

"Great idea. Let's do it. Should I warn MaLeah?"

"Pastor Schaeffer didn't warn you?"

"Good point."

CHAPTER SIX

They all sat down at a First Street Steak House table and began engaging in conversation. After an informal discussion over appetizers, the couples were served a delicious looking meal. Each of the men ordered a steak, while the women ordered chicken.

"I never understood why anyone would order chicken at a steak house." Titus said looking at Owen and Jake.

Owen was trying to find a way to move the casual conversation into a more spiritual area. He launched into it awkwardly, "So Titus, were you nervous about getting baptized this past Sunday?"

"Not too bad."

"Tell them the truth." MaLeah said eyeballing her husband.

"Okay. Yes, I was nervous. It really makes no sense at all. I am in front of people all the time at work. I don't know why I was nervous. I didn't have to say anything. I just had to remember to hold my breath."

Norah laughed and added to the spiritual conversation, "So tell us, what did Pastor Schaeffer say to you at lunch a couple of weeks ago? Owen and I are dying to know."

"He asked me what stood out in the message he had preached." Titus said putting down his fork. "I told him I had felt like I was the one making a bunch of money, but had holes in my pockets. I realized while he was preaching that my life was meaningless. Sure, to the outside world I seemed to be successful. But until I heard Pastor Schaeffer speak, I never realized that my life really meant nothing. For the first time, I realized my god in life was money. So, through the course of our conversation, God convinced me of that sin."

"So, what did you do?" Owen asked, listening intently.

"Pastor Schaeffer asked me if I wanted to repent of my sin and place my faith in Jesus. MaLeah had already done so right there at the table. We had never even said the blessing before a meal, and there she was asking Jesus to be the Lord of her life. And I found myself desiring the same thing."

Norah, wanting to get a little more out of Titus, said, "Well what did you pray."

"I don't remember the prayer word for word. I just remember saying something like, 'God, I am sorry for ignoring you all these years. I have worshipped my money, my job, myself and have totally turned my back on You. But You sent Jesus to die on the cross for my sin, even before I committed it. Please forgive me. Make me a new man today. I want to serve you with all of my heart."

Peggy and Jake looked at one another. They felt extremely out of place. All the spiritual talk was making them a bit uncomfortable. When they thought it couldn't get any worse, MaLeah asked them, "Are you Christians?"

Owen sat back in his chair. He knew MaLeah knew they weren't Christians. He told her on the phone they were trying to share the Gospel with them, too. But Peggy answered. "Not the way you explain it. I always considered myself a Christian just because I live in America. I thought we were all pretty much Christians. But after hearing Titus and you, Norah, last Sunday, I keep thinking to myself, maybe I'm not a Christian."

"What about you, Jake?" Norah probed further.

"I went to church last Sunday. Does that count?"

They all laughed at Jake's comment which seemed to lighten the mood. Titus continued, "I remember Pastor Schaeffer told us at his house that going to church was not the most important thing in life." He had everyone's attention. "The most important thing in life is having a personal relationship with Jesus Christ."

Just then the waitress came to the table and asked, "Sorry to interrupt, but would anyone like dessert?"

"Not me," Owen said. "I'm stuffed."

They all turned down dessert. "Will this be on one check or three?"

"Just put it on one." Titus said. "You can bring that to me."

"Wait a minute. I just met you tonight; you can't pay for my supper." Jake said reaching for his wallet in his back left pocket.

"Don't worry about it. I told Owen this was our treat."

"I appreciate it." Owen said.

"Yeah, thanks a lot. If I would had known you were paying, I would have ordered dessert." Jake said laughing.

The women collected their purses as they all stood up to leave. "When are we going to hit the links again?" Jake asked Owen pulling up his pant legs to show him the PING socks.

"How many pairs of those do you have?" Owen asked laughing as he began sharing the story of those lucky socks with Titus..

"I could beat Owen barefooted." Jake said joking. "What about you, Titus? Do you play?"

"Do I play? I live on a golf course, and I have my own lucky sock collection."

"We should all play together." Owen said.

"Tell me when. We can start on hole number nine behind the house." Titus said.

"The only time I could play would be this Sunday afternoon again."

Owen seized his opportunity. "Tell you what, Jake. You and Peggy come to church again, and we will play after lunch."

"Are you playing golf again?" Norah entered the conversation.

"Mommy, can Owen come out and play Sunday afternoon?" Jake asked Norah in a joking manner.

"I guess so, but he better be home before dark."

As they watched everyone drive away, Norah and Owen did a little victory dance in their car. "It worked!" Norah said with excitement.

"I know. I really thought MaLeah would be the one to share. I never dreamed it would be Titus."

"Pastor Schaeffer was right. They seem like different people."

"We have to let Pastor Schaeffer know what's going on. He will be so fired up he won't know what to do."

"Let's send him a text message." Norah said grabbing Owen's phone out of the cup holder in the car.

"Write: The Gospel ship has set sail!" said Owen cleverly.

She sent the text. Within about two minutes the phone rang. It was Pastor Schaeffer.

"What happened?" he asked.

Owen shared about the evening's events with Pastor. He seemed to get more excited with every sentence Owen shared. "Tell you what. Are you on your way home right now?"

"We sure are."

"Do you have five minutes to stop by our house? Addi and I have something for you."

"Sure, we still have about thirty minutes with the baby sitter."

With excited wonder they drove over to Pastor Schaeffer's house talking about what he might have for them. After hearing a knock on the door, Addi opened it and greeted them with a big smile.

"I didn't get a chance to tell you last Sunday because I was keeping the nursery, how well you did. I heard you through the intercom system downstairs. God used you greatly!"

"Could you hear my knees knocking too?"

"If you were nervous, no one could tell." Pastor Schaeffer affirmed her. "I know you have to go. I just wanted to give you these." He picked up four small boxes: one red, one yellow, one green, and one blue. "You will need these on your journey with Brian and Linda. They already have all the cards inside them. You can figure out a creative way to give them away."

"Do you have an extra refrigerator box?" Owen joked.

"No, but if you go behind Sears and ask for one, they will be glad to give one to you."

"We are so proud of you both. God is doing great things through you. It is so exciting to see Him in action." Addi said as she smiled and hugged them both good-bye.

"We'll see you Sunday. Start praying for Jake and Peggy."

"Oh yeah! How did the golf game go?" Pastor Schaeffer asked.

"Let's not talk about it. I think Jake used to be a golf pro; He stomped me."

They walked out the door with Pastor Schaeffer and Addison waving good-bye. "See you Sunday."

After the door shut, Owen said to Norah, "Wait a minute." He turned around and rang the door bell.

"Did you forget something?" Pastor Schaeffer asked as he opened the door with Addison standing next to him.

"Yeah. One quick question: How do you know so much about the four colors of marriage?"

Pastor Schaeffer looked down at Addi. Addi looked up at him, and they embraced one another. "We've been through all four colors."

APPENDIX

AM Prayer Goals:

> I must choose to change today.
>
> I must choose to fight the real enemy.
>
> I must choose to value my marriage today.

Verses:

> But now you also, put them all aside: anger, wrath, malice, slander and abusive speech from your mouth. Do not lie to one another, since you laid aside the old self with its evil practices, and have put on the new self who is being renewed to a true knowledge according to the image of the one who created Him.—Colossians 3:8-9

> For our struggle is not against flesh and blood, but against the rulers, against the powers, against the world forces of this darkness, against the spiritual forces of wickedness in heavenly places.—Ephesians 6:12

> Marriage is to be held in honor among all and the marriage bed is to be undefiled; for fornicators and adulterers God will punish.—Hebrews 13:4

PM Questions:

> What attitudes and actions have I crucified today?
>
> Have I identified and fought the real enemy today?
>
> How have I shown my spouse I value our marriage today?

AM Prayer Goals:

I will intentionally make marriage a priority today.

I will dwell on that which is good today.

I will make choices which unify our marriage today.

Verses:

Do nothing from selfishness or empty conceit, but with humility of mind regard one another as more important than yourselves.—Philippians 2:3

Finally, brethren, whatever is true, whatever is honorable, whatever is right, whatever is pure, whatever is lovely, whatever is of good repute, if there is any excellence and if anything worthy of praise dwell on these things.—Philippians 4:8

Give preference to one another in honor.—Romans 12:10b

PM Questions:

How have I made my marriage a priority today?

How has my thought life strengthened my marriage today?

How have my choices enhanced the unity of our marriage today?

AM Prayer Goals:

> I will seek to be filled with the Spirit today.
>
> I will seek to serve my spouse today.

Verses:

> And do not get drunk with wine, which is dissipation, but be filled with the Spirit, speaking to one another in psalms and hymns and spiritual songs, singing and making melody with your heart to the Lord; always giving thanks for all things in the name of our Lord Jesus Christ to God, even the Father; and be subject to one another in the fear of Christ.—Ephesians 5:18-21

PM Questions

> Have I crucified my flesh today and given evidence of a Spirit-controlled life?
>
> Have I sought to serve my spouse today?

AM Prayer Goals:

> God, make us a mission-minded couple.
>
> God, make us a mentor-minded couple.

Verses:

> Go therefore and make disciples of all the nations, baptizing them in the name of the Father and the Son and the Holy Spirit, teaching them to observe all that I have commanded you; and lo, I am with you always even to the end of the age.—Matthew 28:19-20
>
> Brethren, even if anyone is caught in any trespass, you who are spiritual, restore such a one in a spirit of gentleness; each one looking to yourself, so that you too will not be tempted.—Galatians 6:1

PM Questions:

> How have my spouse and I prepared to reach out to another couple with the Gospel?
>
> What marriage has God put in our path that we can help grow?